PRE-OWNED
SECOND HAND

WANTED
CASH OR EXCHANGE

BUY · SELL · EXCHANGE · ANY GAUGE · ANY AGE

LOCOS - COACHES - WAGONS - TRACK-WORK - CONTROLLERS - ACCESSORIES
DIE-CAST - LORRIES - BUSES - PLANES - SOLDIERS - RAILWAYANA - AND MORE

DECEASED ESTATES - EX SHOP STOCK A SPECIALITY
FAST SERVICE WITH COMPLETE DISCRETION ASSURED

WE VALUE YOUR COLLECTION VERY HIGHLY!

1 CONTACT US
get in touch by email, phone or post with your list of items

2 OUR OFFER
our friendly staff will review your list and make an honest valuation offer

3 PACKAGE
either visit the shop, send us your items, or we can collect larger collections

4 PAYMENT!
fast, secure payment via your choice on confirming of the value offer – easy!

IMMEDIATE PAYMENT IN 4 EASY STEPS

DON'T DELAY - GET IN TOUCH TODAY!

📞 +44 (0)114 255 1436   ✉ secondhand@railsofsheffield.com

OR VISIT OUR WEBSITE AND CLICK ON THE 💷 Stuff to Sell? LINK:

www.railsofsheffield.com

PROUD WINNERS OF THESE RECENT AWARDS:

What's inside...

MAIN IMAGE: High Weald, an inter-war Southern Railway layout, is one of our featured scenes in our lavish *Masterpieces in the Gallery* feature. JONATHAN NEWTON

RIGHT: The event of the decade, if not the century. The 'Greatest Gathering' in Derby brought together a mass of locomotives to mark 'Railway 200'. Class 37 37401 and Class 47 47739 pose for the camera. There's penty more to enjoy in this yearbook. MIKE WILD

Who did it?

ISBN: 978 1836 3219 34
Editor: Nick Brodrick
Publisher, Modelling: Mike Wild
Senior editor, specials: Roger Mortimer
Email: roger.mortimer@keypublishing.com
Production and design: Panda Media
Cover design: Panda Media
Advertising Sales Manager: Sam Clark
Email: sam.clark@keypublishing.com
Tel: 01780 755131
Advertising production: Becky Antoniades
Email: rebecca.antoniades@keypublishing.com

SUBSCRIPTION/MAIL ORDER
Key Publishing Ltd, PO Box 300, Stamford, Lincs, PE9 1NA
Tel: 01780 480404
Subscriptions email: subs@keypublishing.com
Mail Order email: orders@keypublishing.com
Website: www.keypublishing.com/shop

PUBLISHING
Group CEO: Adrian Cox
Publisher: Steve O'Hara

PUBLISHED BY
Key Publishing Ltd,
PO Box 100, Stamford, Lincs, PE9 1XQ
Tel: 01780 755131
Website: www.keypublishing.com

PRINTING
Melita Press, Paola, Malta

DISTRIBUTION
Seymour Distribution Ltd, 2 Poultry Avenue, London, EC1A 9PU
Enquiries Line: 02074 294000.

Welcome

Welcome to the 201st anniversary of railways! While 2026 might at first appear to be the 'year after the celebrations before' – namely 'Railway 200' – there is no let-up in the excitement, especially for us modellers.

It is appropriate that this yearbook ends on that forward-looking note, as we take stock of the motive power and rolling stock still to come from the major manufacturers following another round of exciting announcements over the last 12 months. The sustainability of continuously launching such vast quantities of ever-increasing quality products has been questioned over the years, with some expecting the bursting of the bubble. Yet it shows no sign of abating – and long may that continue to be the case.

There is no doubt that the spectacular, nationwide celebrations marking the 200th anniversary of the Stockton & Darlington Railway will have helped spark the imagination of the next generation of avid modellers to support that trade.

Here at *Hornby Magazine*, two events will live long in the memory. Firstly, Alstom's 'Greatest Gathering' at Litchurch Lane Works, Derby brought together a quite astonishing number of wheeled exhibits from across the country – believed to be the most ever at a public event. You can relive the August event in full in our yearbook tribute. Derby's Model Railway Village featured the debut of *Hornby Magazine*'s own 'OO' gauge tribute to the Works; built using our exclusive laser cut kits from PJM Models (see pages 92-93 to order yours!).

We moved into the latter part of the year on a similar high with Key Model World's Great Electric Train Show in Milton Keynes.

The magazine team is one to never shirk a challenge, however implausible it might seem. In the days leading up to the October show, we managed to extend our modern image East Coast Cement layout, complete with an all-new station. This collector's edition features the trials and tribulations of how we managed to beat the clock and get the popular tail-chaser to Arena MK – just in the nick of time.

When talking about such nail-biting challenges, it's impossible not to think about Pete Waterman's Making Tracks ventures. We're therefore delighted to catch up with Pete and his fellow 'Railnuts' on these pages to present the latest progress with the modular layout's volume 4+ bringing much enhanced aspects to Watford Junction.

Indeed, 2026 marks the 60th anniversary of the launch of electrified inter-city services through the suburban towns, coinciding with the dramatic modernisation of the West Coast Main Line's Euston station.

We're looking forward to seeing the next steps from Pete Waterman's team, and to a fantastic year ahead including our next Model World LIVE event in April at the NEC in Birmingham.

Happy modelling to you all.

Mike Wild
Publisher, Modelling

Bushey station is one of the latest locations to feature in the Making Tracks series. See pages 20-27 for the full story of its sister layout, Watford Junction.
MIKE WILD

Review of the Year
2024-2025

More than 60 new wheeled models across the five major gauges rolled out of the factories and onto our layouts in the 12 months to autumn 2025. **NICK BRODRICK** recaps another extraordinary period for the hobby.

We have never had it so good. Former Prime Minister Harold McMillan wasn't talking about model railways when he delivered those immortal words his famous speech in 1957, but in our context it certainly rings true.

The 12 months from October 2024 to September 2025 have delivered an extraordinary collection of new model railway announcements spanning all scales, dozens of which passed through *Hornby Magazine* HQ. And rarely, if ever, have we been disappointed. From groundbreaking new toolings to long-awaited prototypes, manufacturers have demonstrated remarkable play value innovation while maintaining exceptional standards of accuracy.

We saw 62 new motive power, carriage and wagon types emerge from 16 manufacturers, bursting our pagination of review pages as

an almost matter of routine. That number doesn't include the sub variants of some of the carriages (such as the four different types of coach in Bachmann's LNWR 'Arc Roof' range).

The breakdown of numbers looks like this…

As fits tradition, 'OO' dominates the scene with three-quarters of all releases. There were 22 new locomotives/multiple units, seven carriage types and 13 wagons.

In 'N', we welcomed two locomotives, one carriage type and 13 wagons, while for 'O', there were seven locomotives/multiple units, one carriage type and one wagon.

The growth of the relatively new 'TT:120's' slowed to just one locomotive release, and it was a relatively quiet year for 'OO9' which saw three passenger rated vans.

So, who'll be most pleased from the year? The evidence suggests that it's 'OO' gauge LNER modelers, who've enjoyed

six locomotives built and absorbed by the company and two very special carriage sets.

More widely, there's been something to please most – and that's what it's all about. Long may it continue!

LOCOMOTIVES
'OO' GAUGE

The timeframe of our survey kicked off with a locomotive that befits the description matchbox. Rapido's North Eastern 'Y7' 0-4-0T might be small, but it is still capable of accepting a Next18 DCC decoder. Introduced by Thomas Worsdell in 1888 and the last handful of engines lasted into early BR service. The little shunting engine won the heart of reviewer Ben Church who described it in HM 211 as "brimming with fine detailing". Ten different liveries have been offered covering NER, LNER and BR eras, as well as National Coal Board engine 6 (with stovepipe rather than the standard fluted chimney).

LEAD AND BELOW: The biggest and smallest steam locomotive releases of the last 12 months are equally impressive Hornby 'OO' *Locomotion No. 1* and Lionheart's '3MT' tank in 'O'. As well as being immortalised in miniature, these two otherwise unconnected designs were memorably posed side-by-side at Derby's Greatest Gathering event in August (see separate feature).

Rapido's reputation for pre-Grouping types continued with its 'Jones Goods' which brought Highland Railway character to the pages of HM212. The David Jones designed 'F' class 4-6-0s (1894-1896) was Britain's first of this wheel arrangement, designed for goods operations in challenging Highland terrain, establishing design principles influencing decades of locomotive development. The model superbly replicates the character of the powerful prototype, down to the louvered chimney of the earlier examples. Four different styles of original HR liveries have been produced (including the as-preserved, 1960s applied yellow on 103, as well as three LMS black styles and a fictional BR-lined black scheme.

Rapido also reissued its splendid Stirling 'Single' No. 1, but this time with its preservation-era Sturrock low sided tender (HM213). Although built with a Stirling water and coal carrier, it gained the anachronistic version in the 1930s when it hauled special trains over LNER metals before entering the National Collection.

Some years after it was first mooted, Rapido delivered its Stroudley 'E1' tank engines, bringing William Stroudley's stout London, Brighton & South Coast Railway 0-6-0T to life (HM 219). The 79-strong class (1874-1891) handled goods and shunting throughout the Brighton network, as well as stretching their use to the Isle of Wight under Southern rule and to the midlands and North East in secondhand industrial use. Models come in 18 different liveries and tooling variations to reflect the many LBSCR, SR, BR and industrial guises the 'E1s' wore during their careers.

An all-new 'Small Prairie' from Rapido delivers an all-new Churchward '4500' for the first time since Bachmann's own effort in 2003. The 2-6-2T is an essential prototype for most GWR branch line situations. Rapido's interpretation of the 175-strong class features a litany of separate fittings, enhancing the overall shape and effective running qualities. As our review in HM220 concluded, whether GWR or BR livery, this 'flat top' 2-6-2T "will find a home on many branch line layouts".

Rapido's sixth new steam offering of the year was the South Eastern & Chatham Railway 'O1' (HM221). The Wainwright 0-6-0 ventures into new pre-Grouping territory for the manufacturer – and to high-acclaim. One of the highlights is the fabulously rendered inside valve gear, which tops off the handsome looks and all-round fidelity. As with most Rapido offerings, there is a full suite of livery options: SECR, SR and BR, plus East Kent Railway and a radical Bluebell Railway lined blue (entirely fictional but very pretty!). The model features a can motor with flywheel, die-cast chassis, pre-fitted dual speakers ready for DCC users, and all-wheel pickups.

Hornby brought its slightly bonkers, yet brilliant, model of *Locomotion No. 1* to the party in good time for the 200th anniversary of the Stockton & Darlington Railway (HM212). The boiler mounted vertical valve gear, varnished wood boiler cladding and plug wheels fully capture this early railway history, modeling George Stephenson's 1825 pioneer as it is now preserved in the national collection.

The Hornby 'J52' is a complete retooling of this Great Northern Railway 0-6-0ST (originally 'J13'), featuring predominantly die-cast construction, strong five-pole motor, function-activated firebox flicker, and

Highland Railway joy for 'OO' collectors with Rapido's superb 'Jones Goods'.

Hornby's best-ever modern image model? Stadler's FLIRT appears in Greater Anglia colours in 'OO'.

HM7000 DCC readiness (HM 219). Despite compact dimensions, it packs sophisticated engineering with space for power bank and changeable lamp codes with the six GNR-stye lamps included. Available in original green, LNER black and BR black, these chunky saddle tanks feature everything their 1980s' Hornby predecessors never could have!

Returning to the North Eastern theme, Oxford Rail's 'J26' emerged as a standout steam release in late 2025, finally bringing these crucial goods lugging machines to ready-to-run availability. Originally designated 'P2' by the NER (later classified 'J26' under the LNER), these Wilson Worsdell-designed 0-6-0s handled heavy freight from 1904-1909. Oxford Rail's model features highly detailed locomotive and tender body shells. Four livery variations cover the operational lifespan: NER lined black, LNER plain black, BR black early, and BR black late.

Hornby steam generator models showcased quite brilliant, synchronised steam and sound effects for the first time on its already high-specification LNER 'A1' and 'P2' and LMS 'Black Five' (HM213).

Accurascale's delightful little 'J67', 'J68' and 'J69' tanks (HM218), designed by James Holden for suburban passenger and light goods duties around London and East Anglia (first classified by the Great Eastern Railway as 'S69'). With 290 locomotives built 1902-1921, they were among Britain's most numerous tank designs, but this is the first time the 0-6-0Ts have featured in RTR 'OO' form. For such a small, boxy model, the detail and range of tooling variations is seriously impressive. The removable cab roof allows a glimpse inside the jeweler's shop-like footplate. Our ranking pronounced the models as "one of the most comprehensive steam locomotives ever produced" which "stand at the pinnacle of 'OO' gauge tank engines".

The OO Works 'J17' addresses one of the remaining gaps for Great Eastern enthusiasts with this 0-6-0 goods design. Over 290 of the Holden engines were built in 1883-1913 served East Anglia under GER, LNER, and BR ownership. These solid hand-built models aren't set-up for plug-and-play DCC users and so would require hard wiring (HM 215).

Accurascale again flexed its muscles in the modern traction market with some dazzling models. Its one-off Class 89, as well as bristling

The Ivatt 'J52' has been a fixture of Hornby catalogues over the decades – and now we have a newly tooled version.

The popular Class 31, now available in 'OO' from Accurascale joining the earlier Bachmann version.

MODEL	SCALE	MANUFACTURER	RELEASED	FEATURED
NER 'Y7' 0-4-0T	'OO'	Rapido Trains UK	November	HM211
SDR Locomotion No. 1	'OO'	Hornby	December	HM212
HR 'Jones Goods' 4-6-0	'OO'	Rapido Trains UK	December	HM212
D600 'Warship' A1A-A1A	'N'	EFE	December	HM212
BR '3MT' 2-6-2T	'O'	Lionheart	December	HM212
GNR Stirling 'Single' 4-2-2	'OO'	Rapido Trains UK	January	HM213
BR HSDT power car	'OO'	Bachmann	January	HM213
Class 66 Co-Co	'TT:120'	Hornby	January	HM213
BR Class 60 Co-Co	'OO'	Cavelex Models	February	HM214
DRS Class 88 Co-Co	'OO'	Dapol	February	HM214
Ruston 88DS 0-4-0DM	'O'	Accurascale	February	HM214
GER 'J17' 0-6-0	'OO'	OO Works	March	HM215
BR Class 31 A1A-A1A	'OO'	Accurascale	March	HM215
BR Class 02 0-4-0DM	'OO'	Heljan	March	HM215
Stadler Class 755 'FLIRT'	'OO'	Hornby	April	HM216
Hunslet 'Austerity' 0-6-0ST	'O'	Dapol	April	HM216
BR Class 24 Bo-Bo	'O'	Heljan	May	HM217
BR Class 02 0-4-0DM	'O'	Heljan	May	HM217
GER 'J69' 0-6-0T	'OO'	Accurascale	June	HM218
BR Class 50 Co-Co	'OO'	Accurascale	June	HM218
BR Class 08/09 0-6-0DM	'OO'	Bachmann	June	HM218
BR Class 44 'Peak' 1Co-Co1	'N'	Rapido Trains UK	June	HM218
BR Class 60 Co-Co	'OO'	Accurascale	July	HM219
LBSCR 'E1' 0-6-0T	'OO'	Rapido Trains UK	July	HM219
GNR 'J52' 0-6-0ST	'OO'	Hornby	July	HM219
GWR '4500' 2-6-2T	'OO'	Rapido Trains UK	August	HM220
BR Class 89 Co-Co	'OO'	Accurascale	August	HM220
Hunslet steelworks Bo-Bo	'OO'	KR Models	August	HM220
SECR 'O1' 0-6-0	'OO'	Rapido Trains UK	September	HM221
NER 'J26' 0-6-0	'OO'	Oxford Rail	September	HM221
BR Class 153 DMU	'O'	Heljan	September	HM221
BR Class 117 DMU	'O'	Heljan	September	HM221

TOTAL: 32

with detail, finally brought the unique 'Badger' to 'OO' gauge with etched metal details, die-cast chassis, and scale-sized Brecknell-Willis pantograph with DCC control. The five-pole motor with twin flywheels and metal helical gearbox achieves scale 125mph top speed. DCC Sound models feature dual-speaker technology. The quality of finish on all five liveried examples – InterCity 'Executive', InterCity 'Swallow', GNER blue with gold lettering, GNER blue with white lettering and as-preserved 'Swallow' – is exceptional, complemented by quartered-polished buffers in its earliest 89001 guise.

Accurascale continued to push the boundaries with its highly impressive A1A-A1A Class 31 (HM215). With more than 65 years in front line main line service, the class has built up a strong following, and these models truly spoil collectors, hot on the heels on Bachmann's own top-notch offering. Like their competitor, the Accurascale models leave no stone unturned in the pursuit of perfection across multiple variants, from the earliest 1950s BR green to Network Rail yellow. The multi-part side frames provide the necessary three-dimensional depth to the bogies which are surrounded by some excellent added detail.

The firm's Class 50 (HM218) brings the famous 'Hoovers' to unprecedented levels of detail for this highly popular class. Built by English Electric 1967-1968, these 2,700hp locomotives became iconic through Western Region passenger services, and on earlier West Coast Main Line pre-electrification runs north of Preston. Features include detailed cab interiors, fine external detailing, powered roof fan that cuts in and out depending on how it is being driven, and authentic sound recordings. Multiple liveries span BR colours (including the unique GWR 150 green 50007 *Sir Edward Elgar*), Network SouthEast and preservation-era schemes (including Hanson + Hall/Rail Adventure's 50008 *Thunderer*).

But if there's one Co-Co that trumps the 'Hoover's heft, it's the Class 60. Accurascale has emulated its reputation for high build quality with its version of the class (HM219),

'Badger' all set! Accurascale's all-new Class 89 is a joy to behold.

The BR diesel that shows no sign of retiring any time soon. Bachmann has superseded its very good early 2000s Class 08/09 shunters with an outstanding one.

featuring die-cast chassis, five-pole motor with flywheel, and comprehensive lighting. Sound-fitted versions – enhanced by the wonderfully named 'Accurathrash' bass speaker – feature authentic recordings from 60 029 hauling 2,500 tons. Visually, the see-through grille into the radiator room showing its cooler group, main air reservoirs and pipework is a real treat.

As if one all-new class Class 60 wasn't enough, Cavelex brought us even more 1989-era power with similarly exceptional specifications (HM214), including 5-pole motor with twin flywheels, photo-etched grilles throughout, and innovative Adaptable Magnetic Detail for rapid customisation allowing the modeller to easily swap bufferbeams between fully detailed and NEM-pockets for tension lock couplings.

The comprehensive lighting package features independently controlled modes including parked, yard, light engine, and 'on train' configurations.

Bachmann's Class 08/09 (HM218) represents a complete reimagining of the earlier 2000 release with entirely new tooling featuring precision molding, die-cast parts, etched metal details, and a five-pole motor delivering excellent slow-speed performance. State-of-the-art lighting includes six individually switchable lights per end plus cab lighting. Flexible tooling allows hundreds of detail combinations reflecting prototype variations: two/four/six lights, radiator steps presence/absence, wooden/steel cab doors, and high-level air pipes. DCC Sound models include Bachmann's clever Auto-Release Coupling and

'Bach-Up' Stay Alive. Liveries span BR Green through DB Cargo Red and Retro BR Blue.

The 'High Speed Diesel Train' from Bachmann ventures into Inter-City 125 territory with the revolutionary power cars (HM213). The prototype 41 001, now in the National Collection, has been captured to a tee. The model comes packed with all the mod-cons you'd expect from a contemporary diesel locomotive (not least lights and sound capability), but the most defining part of the HSDT is its split-screen nose end, that gives it alien like characteristics!

Hornby's FLIRT is a bold, high class move into the East Anglian contemporary scene with these multiple units, capturing the sleek Class 755 units. Described as one of the most feature-packed models Hornby has

The Class 66 is an essential prototype in any scale – and the new army of 'TT:120' modellers will welcome Hornby's varied models into the scale.

Heljan's Class 117 DMU cuts an impressive shape.

ever produced, it features comprehensive lighting (including passenger warning bulbs on doors), HM7000-ready DCC compatibility, and twin five-pole motors. Livery options include Greater Anglia standard, 755/4 variant, 755/3 variant, and the unique Pride livery with rainbow decoration.

KR Models' Bo-Bo steelworks shunter is an off-the-wall subject representing the heavy industry workhorses of industry (HM220). These robust locomotives, employed in steelworks and collieries, are offered in a trio of British Steel colours (green, dark blue and yellow) based Scunthorpe works prototypes. Models display the boxy characteristics of the brutish Hunslet design. Working directional and cab lights are augmented by orange flashing warning lights – a neat touch.

Dapol Class 88 debuts this Stadler Rail electro-diesel for Direct Rail Services, representing the UK's first 25kV AC dual-mode locomotive (HM214). This all-new model has been developed by Dapol exclusively for Rails of Sheffield and makes a perfect partner to Dapol's already established and popular Class 68 with which the real Class 88s share many parts. Features include finely moulded body with separately fitted details, heavy die-cast chassis with all-wheel pickup/drive, smooth five-pole motor with twin flywheels, and comprehensive lighting (marker/headlights, tail lights, halo lights, cab lights – all independently DCC controllable). The servo-controlled pantograph operates under DCC too. Just like the real '88', this model is powerful and sure-footed.

Heljan's Class 02 brings Clayton Equipment Company's little 180hp Paxman-engine design to 'OO'. Built in 1959-1961, primarily to replace the ageing Horwich 'Pug' 0-4-0STs, only 20 locomotives were constructed, making them relatively rare prototypes adding character to diesel-era layouts with distinctive styling suited for shunting duties. At first glance, the design is outwardly simple but take a closer look and you'll see a wealth of separately fitted details that elevate this titchy model (HM215).

'N' GAUGE

EFE's D600 'Warship' addresses Western Region diesel hydraulic enthusiasts (HM 212). The A1A-A1A type represented the early British development of German hydraulic

transmission technology, creating distinctive powerful locomotives serving Western Region express services until premature early-1970s withdrawal. The hunched look of the real thing has been well captured in this small form, with its liberal coating of grills, panels, hatches, doors and rivet detailing. Cab and directional lights add the final flourish to this little gem which is almost the equal of its 'OO' equivalent from the same manufacturer.

Rapido's only second dip into British 'N' gauge motive power brings 'Peak' power with excellent power and detail characteristics. The Class 44 (HM218) is the first of three variants to be offered ('45' and '46' the others). Nine liveries spanning BR green and blue have been offered as part of this initial batch, offering a wealth of tiny separately fitted parts. There's also full sound specification for digital users.

'O' GAUGE

The Lionheart '3MT' 2-6-2T brings this chunky British Railways standard design to an exceptional level of detail in 'O' (HM212). Laced with detail fittings, this hefty tank engine benefits from an ideal blend of die-cast metal, etched brass and injection moulded plastic parts. Both BR green and black liveries are available in both early and late crest.

This larger scale is particularly popular for shunting layouts and what better locomotive for an industrial setting than the ubiquitous Austerity 0-6-0ST? Dapol has come up trumps with the clean yet bulky lines of its War Department design (HM216), which truly excels for its working inside motion that is readily visible between the frames in the expanse of daylight below the boiler. Ten different liveries have been produced so far: four industrial, one Longmoor Military Railway blue, one LNER 'J94' and three BR 'J94s'.

Accurascale also ventured into industrial territory and 'O' gauge with the Ruston 88DS (HM214), providing crucial motive power for industrial, private railway and BR departmental modelling. The four-wheel locomotives saw widespread use from the late 1930s well into the privatised era providing reliable economic power. Though a far more basic prototype design than what Accurascale typically offers, it has captured these little diesel shunters to aplomb.

The Heljan Class 153 achieves success in bringing more modern DMUs to larger scale (HM221). Based on original research with Porterbrook Leasing assistance, features include factory-fitted speakers, illuminated door locking/button lights, cab/saloon interior lighting, and prototypical route/destination displays. Six liveries are available: Regional Railways, Stagecoach East Midlands, Northern 'Swoosh', Transport for Wales grey/red, London Midland City, and GWR Green. Taking full advantage of the larger scale, Heljan has included some nifty touches, like leaving some of the hopper windows in the open position. Lights and sounds are there too, naturally. And if you're into DCC, don't be surprised to hear the earworm 'Say it, see it, sorted'!

The BR Class 24s represented early BR diesel development, serving late-1950s through 1980s in various roles. An important gap therefore for someone to fill, and it was Heljan who served up

Gresley articulation 'Quad Art' style from Clark Railworks...

the 'Rats' in 2025. The Danes have again excelled in this gauge with a model that combines finesse and heft, plus all the bells and whistles you'd expect – lights, sound and powered roof fan (all DCC controllable).

At the opposite end of the scale is the Class 02 diesel shunter (HM217), matching Heljan's simultaneous release of the Yorkshire Engine Company type in 'OO'. Good use of die cast metal has been made for the chunky bits of the model, namely bodyshell and chassis, meaning the barely 6in long '02' has enough tractive effort at least as anything you'd reasonably expect from it to pull and push around sidings. As with its smaller sister, there isn't an awful lot of detail to take in given the simple nature of the real thing, but what there is has been very nicely captured.

A strong 12 months in 7mm scale for Heljan is rounded off with the two- and three-car Class 117 DMU (HM217), bringing important cross-country units serving Western Region suburban and cross-country services, and Fife Circle commuter trains in the 1990s. The profile of the units has been recreated to great effect, complemented by a host of smaller fittings – inside and out. Particularly

impressive is that the underframe has been modelled in full relief. Liveries already available are BR green (with whiskers and yellow warning panel), BR blue and grey, BR blue and Network SouthEast.

'TT:120' SCALE

In the words of Key's Publisher for Modelling Mike Wild, the new Hornby Class 66 is "well placed to lead the world of 'TT:120' into the modern era" (HM213). Despite its small size, there are a host of tooling options available from the earliest turn of the century EWS/DB Cargo '66s' right through to GBRf's latest '66/7s'. Myriad small parts adorn these smashing locomotives, which also offer DCC sound and directional lighting, offered in night and day modes. With high quality 'Sheds' available in 'N', 'OO' and 'O', it's only right that we now have one for 'TT:120' too!

CARRIAGES
'OO' GAUGE

Hornby's 'Coronation' coaches arguably represent the 'wow' release for coaching stock in 2025 (HM211). Operating on the prestigious London – Edinburgh 'Coronation'

... and 'Coronation' fashion from Hornby.

A most welcome addition in 2025 was Bachmann's exquisite LNWR 'Arc Roof' main line stock.

express, this stock featured 1930s streamlined styling, advanced articulated bogies for smooth high-speed running, and luxurious ocean-liner-rivaling interiors. The coaches are simply stunning: the chromed beading and lettering are an appropriate finishing touch. There are fully detailed interiors (with lighting of course) and rubber streamlining baffles that fit between vehicles. And the splendid 'Beavertail' observation car is a must-have addition.

Bachmann's LNWR 'Arc Roof' stock (HM217) will delight pre-grouping enthusiasts with Victorian-era passenger vehicles. The types display plenty of cosmetic features across the three stylish liveries: LNWR plum and spilt milk, LMS crimson and Midland & Great Northern Joint Railway brown, all in four different types – Tri-Composite, Brake Composite, Third and Full Brake. Other than Southern constituent designs and generic pre-Grouping vehicles, the 'Arcs' represent a rare venture into the pre-1923 world of main line and secondary route carriages in 'OO' – and for that these are most welcome.

Bachmann reworked Mk 1s – namely the Brake Second Open, First Open and Restaurant Buffet – brings some welcome tweaks, including retooled bogies (HM212).

Accurascale produced nine types of BR's well-travelled late 1960s-early 1970s successor to the Mk 1 – the Mk 2c stock (HM214). These new coaches come with full LED-lit interiors, anti-flicker capacitors, and all-wheel pickups with magnetic wand control. Features include die-cast chassis, accurate BR4 bogies with separate detailing, blackened wheels, scale wire handrails, separately fitted door handles/lamp brackets, fully detailed die-cast underframes, and prism-free flush glazing. Core liveries offered so fare are BR blue and grey, Trans-Pennine, Regional Railways, Network SouthEast and West Coast Railways.

Rapido's 'B-Set' (HM214) brings 1930s Great Western Railway passenger stock which, like autocoaches, are essential items for branch line layouts. These coaches feature distinctive bow styling on the ends and tumblehomes which have been nicely replicated in 'OO' form. Aside from the usual array of details, these models score highly on two things in particular – the etched luggage racks and spare droplights to model windows in the open position if desired. Liveries span GWR chocolate and cream (two variants), wartime brown, BR crimson, BR maroon (plain and lined) and BR chocolate and cream.

The Dapol Black Label Q13 Inspection Saloon (HM221) offers Hawksworth's distinctive Western Region design with premium Black Label series specification, incorporating enhanced detailing and features reflecting the higher market segment standards. Lighting (controllable under DCC control) allows the populated interior saloon and lounge to be fully appreciated, and exterior detail has not been skimped on either.

Clark Railworks has entered the 'OO' carriage market and boldly selected the LNER Gresley 'Quad Arts' as its starting point (HM217). These articulated coaches come as fixed-four coach rakes, but in separate matching 'A' and 'B' packs to make up a complete eight carriage set. As well as sharing bogies, the coaches are distinctive for having so many doors and windows – reflecting their heigh capacity suburban style. These superb models include lighting and interior compartment detail, most notably luggage racks and artistic picture frames. It seems only a matter of time before a modern standard Gresley 'N2' is produced to haul them.

'N' GAUGE

Graham Farish's Mk 1 Post Office Tender joined the range to complement the extant Post Office Sorting Vans in both Royal Mail red and BR blue and grey (HM217).

Revolution Trains stepped forward with an unusual, but most welcome, vehicle in the shape of Caroline – the former Southern Region General Manager's Inspection Saloon (HM211). The finesse and detailing of this rebuilt 'Hastings DEMU' buffet car must be seen to be believed.

'O' GAUGE

Ellis Clark Trains' all new K-Type Pullmans (HM213) bring luxury travel to 'O' gauge. Pullman cars defined British railway passenger accommodation pinnacle, featuring sumptuous interiors, and their distinctive brown and cream liveries. These stunning models reflect every inch of that pride, containing a wealth of finesse that is possibly unsurpassed in mainstream RTR rolling stock. There's etched brass luggage

2025-2026 NEW READY TO RUN CARRIAGES

MODEL	SCALE	MANUFACTURER	RELEASED	FEATURED
LNER 'Coronation' stock	'OO'	Hornby	November	HM211
Ffestiniog 'Tin Car' stock	'OO9'	Bachmann	November	HM211
Ffestiniog brake third bogie van	'OO9'	Bachmann	December	HM212
Pullman stock – K-Type	'O'	Ellis Clark Trains	December	HM213
GWR 'B-Set'	'OO'	Rapido Trains UK	January	HM214
BR Mk 2c stock	'OO'	Accurascale	January	HM214
LNWR 'Arc Roof' stock	'OO'	Bachmann	May	HM217
Ffestiniog 'Curly Roof' van	'OO9'	Bachmann	May	HM217
LNER 'Quad Arts'	'OO'	Clark Railworks	May	HM217
BR Mk 1 (BSO, FO, RB)	'OO'	Bachmann	May	HM217
Mk 1 Post Office Tender	'N'	Graham Farish	May	HM217
BR(W) Q13 Inspection Saloon	'OO'	Dapol	September	HM221

TOTAL: 12

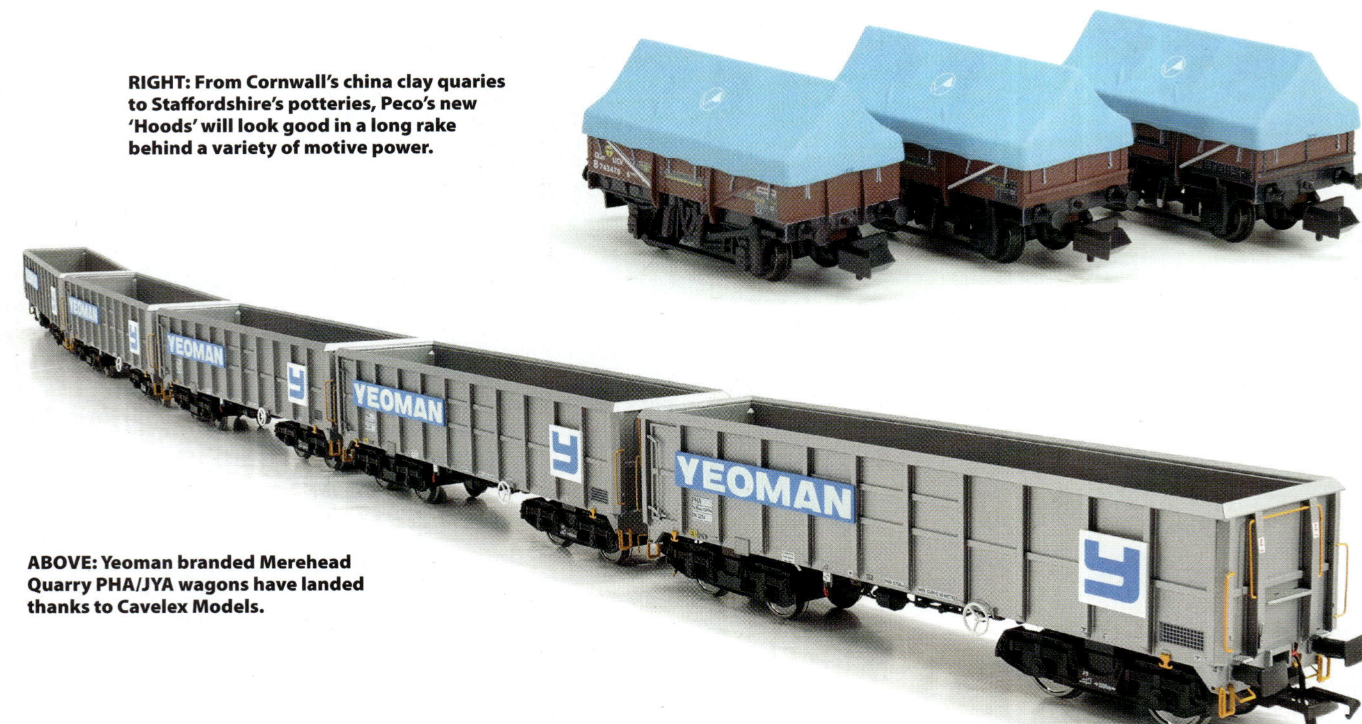

RIGHT: From Cornwall's china clay quaries to Staffordshire's potteries, Peco's new 'Hoods' will look good in a long rake behind a variety of motive power.

ABOVE: Yeoman branded Merehead Quarry PHA/JYA wagons have landed thanks to Cavelex Models.

racks, printed carpets, lamps (working) and even dinner service menus for tables. Construction is of high standard – etched brass sides and injection moulded ends, together with superb livery application.

'OO9' GAUGE

Bachmann curly roof van (HM217), brake third bogie van (HM212) and 1970s 'Tin Car' (HM211) carriages are the latest in a long line of contemporary Ffestiniog Railway vehicles for the 'OO9' narrow gauge market. All superbly detailed, as you'd expect!

WAGONS
'OO' GAUGE

Modern image modellers benefitted from the arrival of the compact Theurer 12tonne GPC72 General Purpose Crane from EFE (HM211). These contemporary track work vehicles, which first emerged in the late 1970s, do not come with working arm and jib, but give every impression of being *capable* of being so.

All new four-wheel 'Palvans' from Bachmann (HM212) fill a key gap in the ranks of steam-era vans, with plenty of separate handrail detail and different underframe tooling variants allowing for later versions to be modelled.

Accurascale's 16-ton mineral wagons (HM213) are an excellent represention the largest freight category serving collieries, power stations, quarries, and industrial operations. Models, made with moulded plastic bodies and die cast chassis, are available as triple wagon packs across 20 variants (BR, NCB and private owner).

From 16-ton opens to 21-ton hoppers, there was yet more BR wagon goodies in store from Accurscale in the pages of HM218. Based on LNER design, these new types are particularly handy for BR blue era layouts. As you'd envisage, they are incredibly highly detailed. Available in BR and industrial colours, they come in packs of three.

Kernow Model Centre's LBSCR opens (HM213) are similarly first-rate models with an attractive

array of separate brake linkages, couplings and brake handle safety chains. Suitable for pre-Grouping, SR and BR eras, they come in high-bar and standard variations.

Modern Merehead quarry runs can be faithfully recreated thanks to Cavelex Models' (Ultimate Model Railways) PHA/JYA wagons (HM214). Available in single and five wagon packs, these Yeoman branded bogie opens smothered in small parts and an excellent finish.

Revolution IHA-F wagons (HM216) are another terrific offering from Revolution Trains; the French-built steel carrying bogie wagons boasting a plastic cover that has been expertly made to look just like draped canvass over steel ribbing.

Fish vans were another debut subject for Rapido (HM216). Its BR Diagram 1/801 are

offered in multiple versions to cover their full lifespan: Blue Spot, 'Ice Blue', Parcels SPV, Parcels NRV, Barrier vans, and Departmental.

The Canadian firm's Diagram 67 van (HM216) ventures into Scottish railway territory with distinctive pre-grouping design of the Caledonian Railway. The cross-braced bodies come in a assortment of branded colours.

Rapido's double GWR offering of the O18 5-plank and N19 (HM215) steel-bodied open wagons (the latter for transporting locomotive coal) are to its typically crisp, high standard.

LMS fans welcomed Hornby's 'Salmon' rail carriers to the range (HM218). These ostensibly simple designs have been well represented in both their original timber floor and later flush topped construction.

BR 16-ton 'minerals' arrived from Accurascale.

LEFT: It's been another bumper crop of 'OO9' models for Ffestiniog Railway enthusiasts. This is the quirky 'Curly Roof' van.

ABOVE: Revolution Trains' Cartic-4s in 'N' are suitable for mid-1960s layouts onwards.

Dapol's substantial ARC/JHA wagons (HM218) are most welcome match to the company's earlier Class 59 diesels, carrying the muted mustardy Amey Roadstone Contruction livery. Full internal detail of the hoppers is supplemented by a wonderful array of fixtures on the underframe.

BR's demountable tank wagons were originally built for brewery produce with removable crane-lifted tank units. They were adapted for carrying other unusual loads, like propellers. Clark Railworks' unusual models (HM221) feature die-cast chassis, removable loads and sprung buffers.

'N' GAUGE

Revolution IHA-F brings modern steel carriers from 'OO' to this smaller scale (HM218) with no appreciable downgrading of detail or decoration. These will really look the 'biz' in long formations.

Although modern-looking, Revolution Trains Cartic-4's can be justifiably described as a steam-era addition in 'N' (HM215).

The earliest Motorail versions are ideal for post 1964-era modellers, while the later refurbished versions with 'Expamet' screens are ideal for the modern era. It's up to the consumer to add the new cars of their choice (if any)!

Peco newly-tooled china clay 'hood' wagons (HM215) represent the 9ft underframe GWR/BR 'Clay-Tip' wagons from late 1940s/early 1950s, originally using flat tarpaulins, and the later mid-1970s 'tent' covers in sky blue. They are available in BR Bauxite representing UCV and OOV classifications across different periods.

Rapido continued to show growth in the small scale with its BR Diagram 1/191 'OOA' opens (HM211), complementing its earlier 'OO' offering. Triple packs are available in bauxite, Railfreight red and grey, Civil Link grey and yellow, and EWS red and gold.

'O' GAUGE

The Heljan 'PMV' delivers postal operations to 'O' gauge (HM215). These Southern Railway Parcels and Miscellaneous Vans embody one of the most recognizable utility vehicles used from the 1920s-well into the BR blue era. The newly tooled models cover wide detail variations: even planked, uneven planked, and plywood bodied options with corresponding door variations. Features include high detail levels, compensated axles, sprung screw link couplings, and sprung buffers.

OVERALL

Phew. Well, what a year. *Again!*

The 12 months from September 2024 to September 2025 have been exceptional for us modellers. Yes, it might have been a relatively quiet year for coaching stock across all gauges, but that's been more than made up by the sheer quality and diversity of what's been offered in so many ways.

We live in exciting times for railway modellers across all scales and interests. Can 2025-2026 top this one? Watch this space! ∎

2025-2026 NEW READY TO RUN WAGONS				
MODEL	SCALE	MANUFACTURER	RELEASED	FEATURED
Theurer 12tonne GPC72 crane	'OO'	EFE	November	HM211
BR Diagram 1/191 'OOA'	'N'	Rapido Trains UK	November	HM211
BR 'Palvan'	'OO'	Bachmann	December	HM212
LBSCR open wagon	'OO'	Kernow Model Centre	January	HM213
BR 16-ton mineral wagon	'OO'	Accurascale	January	HM213
PHA/JYA hopper	'OO'	Cavelex Models	February	HM214
GWR O18 open	'OO'	Rapido Trains UK	March	HM215
GWR N19 open	'OO'	Rapido Trains UK	March	HM215
GWR/BR china clay 9ft open	'N'	Peco	March	HM215
Cartic-4 car transporter	'N'	Revolution Trains	March	HM215
SR 'PMV'	'O'	Heljan	March	HM215
CR Diagram 67 van	'OO'	Rapido Trains UK	April	HM216
BR Diagram 1/801 fish van	'OO'	Rapido Trains UK	April	HM216
IHA-F steel carrying wagon	'OO'	Revolution Trains	April	HM216
LMS 'Salmon' rail carrier	'OO'	Hornby	June	HM218
ARC/JHA stone hopper	'OO'	Dapol	June	HM218
IHA-F steel carrying wagon	'N'	Revolution Trains	June	HM218
BR demountable tank wagon	'OO'	Clark Railworks	September	HM221

TOTAL: 18

SUBSCRIBE TODAY!

WHICH *HORNBY MAGAZINE* SUBSCRIPTION SUITS YOU BEST?

A | 12 MONTH SUBSCRIPTION

BEST VALUE

UK PRINT - 1 year

£59.99*

Paying by Annual Direct Debit

PLUS A FREE GIFT!

B | 6 MONTH SUBSCRIPTION

UK PRINT - 6 months

£31.00

Paying by 6-Month Direct Debit

PLUS A FREE GIFT!

FREE GIFT

WORTH £17.99!

Hornby Yearbook 2025

The Hardback version of the 2025 Hornby Magazine Yearbook is the must have annual to suit almost every modelling taste and ability.

Packed with in-depth modelling guides, top notch photography, awe inspiring projects, and a full mainstream manufacturers' review of the year.

The 17th edition of this popular yearbook contains exclusive material from the Hornby Magazine's expert team, as well as unseen material from Britain's best modellers in a wide range of scales, traction and eras.

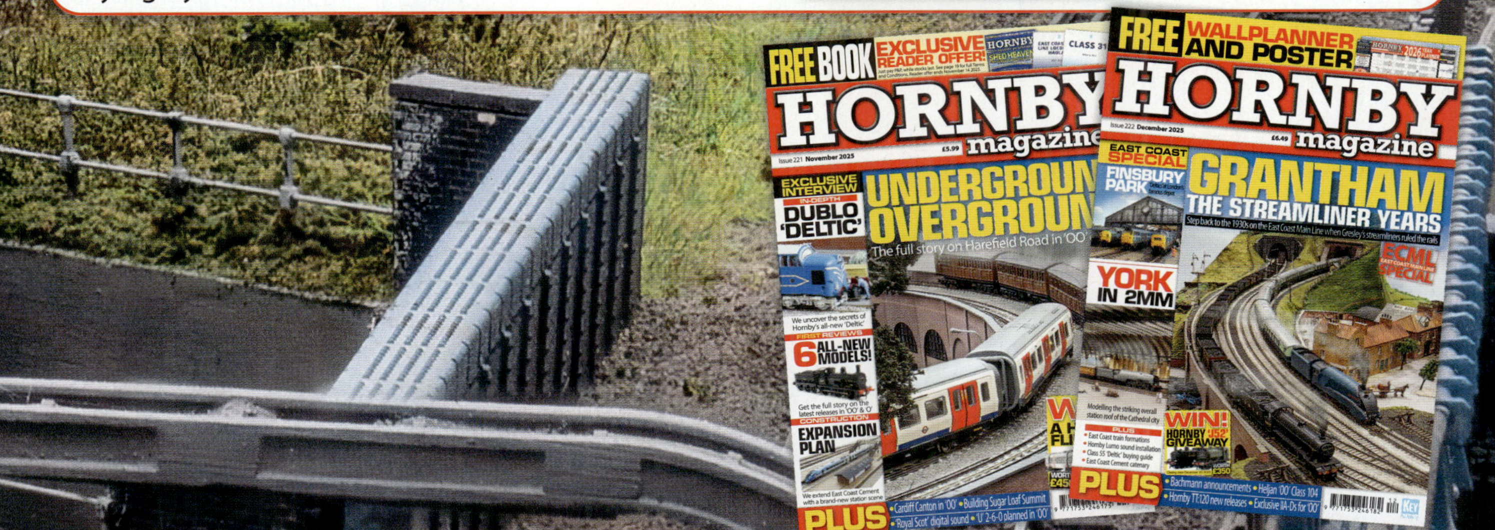

REASONS TO SUBSCRIBE TO *HORNBY MAGAZINE*..

» **EXCLUSIVE** Subscriber offers across books, specials, limited editions and modelling essentials » **SAVE** - *Hornby Magazine* subscribers can **SAVE £20** on Railway Touring Company main line steam trip tickets! » **NEVER MISS AN ISSUE** - delivered direct to your door every month » **DISCOUNTS** on The Great Electric Train Show and Model World LIVE event tickets » **BE THE FIRST** to read the latest features » **FREE GIFT** for new UK print 1 year subscriptions

MAKING TRACKS 4+

WATFORD JUNCTION

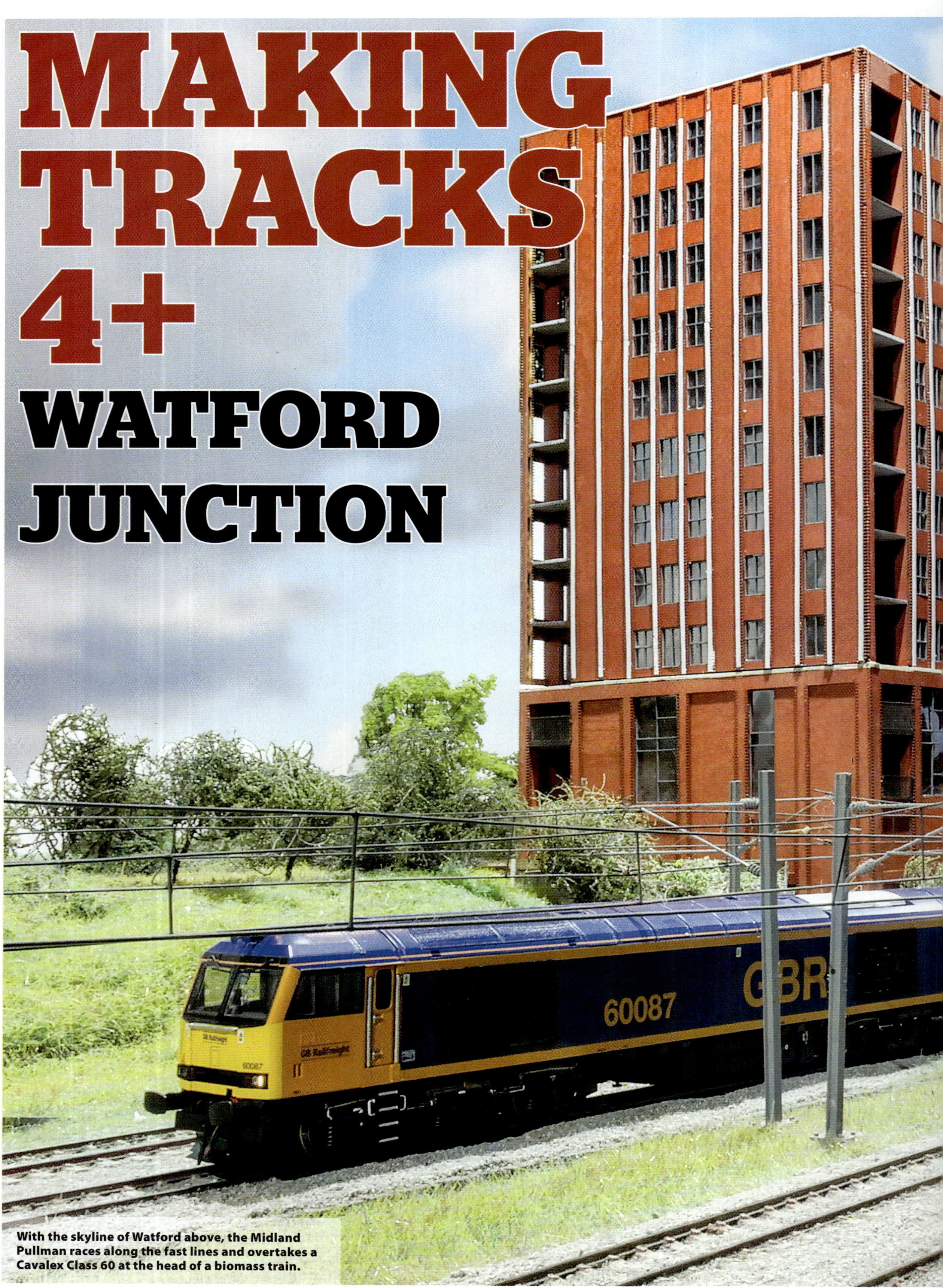

With the skyline of Watford above, the Midland Pullman races along the fast lines and overtakes a Cavalex Class 60 at the head of a biomass train.

Pete Waterman and the Railnuts set themselves a new challenge to expand Watford Junction in time for Model World LIVE on April 26/27 2025. **MIKE WILD** explains all about the layout which won the 2025 Layout of the Year in the *Hornby Magazine* Model Railway Awards.

Laser-cut buildings have been created to model Watford around the railway. A Class 390 rushes north on the fast lines as a Class 88 and Class 37 pass on the slow.

Key Publishing's exclusive Accurascale limited edition sample of Class 66 66794 *Steve Hannam* heads a rake of Revolution Trains JNA-T wagons past the most complex of the flats built for the layout.

There is no stopping Pete Waterman and the Railnuts. No sooner have they completed one part of Making Tracks then there is a plan to develop it further or build a new section. 2025 has been another busy year for the group with appearances across the year including Model World LIVE in April 2025 with Watford Junction.

The 'OO' gauge model of Watford Junction, now known as Making Tracks 4+, has been progressively developed over the past 12 months – and amazingly a year ago, this layout was still incomplete ahead of the Guinness World Records challenge to create the Largest Portable Model Railway at Model World LIVE in April 2024.

Since then, it has been modified so it can operate as a solo layout and made its debut in 64ft x 12ft form at Chester Cathedral in summer 2024. There the models of Bushey Viaduct, Watford Junction's main line station platforms and Watford Tunnel were joined by a new scene based on Roade Cutting to turn it into a continuous run layout of its own. During the month-long exhibition in the Cathedral, the team started the next big challenge which was to expand Watford Junction to feature more of the scenery around the railway, much as they did with Milton Keynes Central in 2023. This time, the plan was to model the huge 20-storey high flats which are currently approaching completion at the real location as well as the distinctive office block above the station entrance.

These features were completed for the 2024 Great Electric Train Show on October 12/13 where Watford Junction took on a whole new appearance, but time meant that only two of the three flats were complete and the Railnuts wanted to introduce the car park and daycare centre behind Watford Junction station to continue recreating the station and its environment in miniature.

Fast forward to December 2024 and the layout was on display at Cheshire Outdoors for Making Tracks at Christmas by which time the third block of flats had been completed and the baseboards for the scene rebuilt and rearranged to allow those missing features – the car park and daycare centre – to be modelled too, presenting the best recreation of Watford Junction station in 'OO' gauge so far.

ADDING THE PLUS

At the start of 2025, Pete Waterman and the team were beginning their preparations for the year ahead which saw Making Tracks layouts on display at Model World LIVE on April 26/27 2025, The Greatest Gathering at Alstom's Derby Litchurch Lane Works on August 1-3 2025, Chester Cathedral in August 2025, at the Great Electric Train Show on October 11/12 2025 and finally at the Vale of Rheidol Railway from October 25-November 3. During the year they will be showing two different layouts with the final call in Aberystwyth bringing together all of the layouts once more to reassemble the 208ft x 14ft layout for full testing.

Moving back to Watford Junction, it has been displayed in the usual 64ft length that fitted into Chester Cathedral, but during early 2025 it was extended by 8ft, hence the name Making Tracks 4+. That might not seem like much, but it wasn't just the length that was extended – it also doubled the width at that point while four brand-new structures were created which pushed the boundaries of what can be achieved in the time available, and with modern technology.

The new buildings model a trio of flats east of the main line as it heads north towards Watford Tunnel. Each of the buildings is unique and required a laser-cut 'kit' of parts to be drawn in 3D CAD and then cut. It sounds deceptively simple, but more than 200 hours were invested in drawing the first and most complex of the three large buildings and in all it will have more than 500 parts which had to be assembled and painted to create the final model.

These buildings continue the high-rise theme as the Railnuts model the skyline at Watford Junction in 'OO' gauge to present an

The station features scale length platforms as well as scale trees made by Pete Waterman to stand alongside the huge buildings. A Class 60 leads a rake of PHA bogie wagons north along the West Coast Main Line.

image of the real railway in miniature which is rare on the exhibition circuit. However, the impact isn't really appreciated until you see it in the flesh. The size and scope of the buildings is something else. The tallest is 22 stories high and almost a metre high on its own. It sits on a baseboard already a metre off the ground which adds even more to its status and appearance.

These buildings dominate the trains and even full-length Pendolinos and container trains are dwarfed by the structures around them and become part of the scene rather than the focus. It's a completely different way of modelling the railway and by modelling it as near to scale as possible shows how everything fits together.

The result of all this will be a sense of scale that you seldom see in exhibition layouts. Watford Junction now has scale length platforms capable of hosting an 11-coach Pendolino at more than 13ft long, scenery which expands to almost 7ft across at its widest point and, if that wasn't enough, towering structures behind which even the tallest Railnut member needs a 6ft ladder to assemble when it goes out on the road. All of which is portable.

Making Tracks 4+ is stunning layout and represents a different way of modelling the railway. It was voted as the 2025 Layout of the Year in the Hornby Magazine Model Railway Awards – an award which was presented to Pete Waterman and the Railnuts at the 2025 Great Electric Train Show. Congratulations to the team and we can't wait to see what's next. ∎

Double-headed Freightliner Class 90 take a container train south on the approach to Watford Junction station.

The complex shapes of the new flats alongside the main road were one of the biggest challenges. It took over 200 hours of design work to create this structure.

The New Measurement Train is powered by Key Publishing's exclusive Hornby limited edition livery samples of 43277 *Safety Task Force* and 43257 running beneath the wires.

These four new structures expanded the skyline on the approach to Watford. In the foreground is the original London and Birmingham Railway station building which still stands today.

DERBY'S GREATEST DAYS

'Railway 200' might have celebrated the opening of the Stockton & Darlington Railway, but the most spectacular event took place in the East Midlands. **NICK BRODRICK** presents the highlights of Britain's biggest ever railway show.

T

he Greatest Gathering at Alstom's Derby Litchurch Lane Works proved to be the of the most remarkable railway heritage events ever staged in Britain.

The unprecedented scale of August 1-3 2025 celebration brought together the world's largest collection of historic and modern rolling stock to commemorate 200 years of the modern railway at Britain's oldest continually operating train factory. The site was transformed into a living museum of railway history, drawing enthusiasts from across the globe to witness this once-in-a-lifetime event.

Rob Whyte, Alstom's UK Managing Director, described it as "the world's largest-ever gathering of historic and modern trains and rail-related exhibits".

The event formed the centrepiece of 'Railway 200', marking the bicentenary of George Stephenson's pioneering achievement when *Locomotion No. 1* hauled the first public railway passengers on the Stockton and Darlington Railway on 27 September 1825.

The open weekend had local significance too. The 90-acre Litchurch Lane site – Britain's largest railway factory – was opened by the Midland Railway in 1876 and provided a unique backdrop as the only UK facility that still designs, engineers, builds and tests trains for both domestic and export markets. This historical continuity, spanning nearly 150 years of railway manufacturing, added profound meaning to the bicentenary celebrations.

Over 40,000 enthusiasts descended on Derby across the three days, with visitors travelling from as far as New Zealand, Japan, and North America. Many international visitors planned entire holidays around the event. Event co-organiser Ben Goodwin

MAIN: Just some of the galaxy of steam stars: *Flying Scotsman, Bahamas* **and** *Blue Peter*. **NICK BRODRICK.**

TOP: SouthEastern's Network SouthEast-inspired 'Networker' *Chris Green* **shares shed space with a Class 507 and other EMUs. MIKE WILD.**

"The event formed the centrepiece of Railway 200, marking the bicentenary of George Stephenson's pioneering achievement"

declared it "a resounding success", receiving "reams and reams of just beautiful, wonderful comments". The gathering raised significant funds for Railway Children, the charity supporting vulnerable children across transport networks, with over £250,000 collected through ticket sales, donations, and special fundraising activities across the weekend.

Alstom's Rob Whyte reflected that the event was "a once-in-a-generation celebration of Britain's railway heritage and future" that "simply wouldn't have been possible without the extraordinary support of so many".

STEAM SPECTACULAR

Naturally, it was LNER Gresley 'A3' 4-6-2 60103 *Flying Scotsman* – reckoned to be the world's most famous powered object on wheels – that took centre stage. Its appearance was confirmed just weeks before the event, with Alstom releasing additional 2,500 tickets per

Locomotion No 1 – the reason we're all here – is displayed in G Shop with part-built '3MT' 82045. NICK BRODRICK.

Eurostar Class 373 power car 3999 lines up alongside Class 43 HST power car 43004, Class 390 'Pendolino' 390119, Class 91 91105 and 'Deltic' D9009 representing high speed rail travel from 1961 to the present day. MIKE WILD.

Four of the five '50s', from left: 50035 *Ark Royal*, 50007 Hercules, 50033, *Glorious* and 50049 *Defiance*. NICK BRODRICK.

day to celebrate its attendance on top of the 30,000 total already allocated.

Joining it was a trio of other 'Pacifics' to complete a royal flush of East Coast Main Line steam motive power: 'A4' 60007 *Sir Nigel Gresley*, Peppercorn 'A1' 60163 *Tornado* and 'A2' 60532 *Blue Peter*.

Derby's own locomotive heritage featured prominently through LMS 'Compound' 4-4-0 1000, built at the city's former Locomotive Works in 1902 and preserved as part of the national collection. Another, newer Derby stalwart came in the form of Caprotti valve-gear BR Standard '5MT' 73129.

Being in the heart of London Midland Region territory, there was logically a bias towards ex-LMS products: ex-LNWR 'Coal Tank' 1054, 'Mogul 13268, 'Royal Scot' 46115 *Scots Guardsman*, 'Jubilees' 45596 *Bahamas* and 45699 *Galatea*, 'Black Five' 44932 and 'Princess Royal' 46203 *Princess Margaret Rose*. And as a constituent company of the LMS, there was further interest in the shape of Britain's oldest working standard gauge locomotive – Furness Railway 0-4-0 20.

Southern power was represented by two Bulleid 'Merchant Navies', 35018 *British India Line* and 35028 *Clan Line*, while 'Hall' 4930 *Hagley Hall* and 'King' 6023 *King Edward II* flew the flag for the GWR.

And an event inspired by the S&DR wouldn't be complete without the locomotive, or rather *Locomotion*, itself. The fragile surviving (albeit much-rebuilt) Stephenson 0-4-0 of 1825 was making an extremely rare visit away from the North East for the gathering. It was nattily displayed alongside a technically extinct class of locomotive – part-built replica BR '3MT' 82045

TOP LEFT: Cab access was provided to many exhibits, including *British India Line* and *Clan Line*. NICK BRODRICK.
TOP RIGHT: The Model Railway Village, in association with Key Model World, was teeming with people. JONATHAN NEWTON.
ABOVE: Bringing up the 'Baby'! The largely complete replica Class 23 D5910 in Works grey. MIKE WILD.

Spotter's paradise! A '27', '26', three '57s' and a '66' fill Stephenson Way. MIKE WILD.

'Badger' and 'Dyson'.
MIKE WILD.

from the Severn Valley Railway.

Nor was it only standard gauge… There were miniature train rides, and 2ft gauge shuttles with Ffestiniog Rialway 0-4-4STT *Prince* and Trangkil Sugar Mill 0-4-2T running in top and tail mode.

MODERN MANIA

The transition from steam was illustrated through an exceptional collection of preserved diesels. Class 55 Deltic D9000 *Royal Scots Grey* appeared - the first of its class that introduced 100mph passenger services to the British network in 1961. The BR blue Class 55 appeared alongside D9015 *Tulyar*, making its first-post overhaul appearances.

The Western Region's diesel-hydraulic tradition lived on through Class 52 D1015 *Western Champion*.

The Class 50 Alliance brought an impressive gathering of *five* examples from the class, wearing variations of BR blue and, uniquely, Greatest Gathering vinyl wraps.

The sheer variety of diesel traction was stunning, with at least one representative from Classes 08, 11, 17, 23, 26, 27, 31, 33, 35, 37, 40, 42, 44, 45, 46, 50, 52, 55 and 56.

If the Class 23 isn't overly familiar, that's because it is the largely complete new build 'Baby Deltic', making its first ever foray outside Barrow Hill Roundhouse.

Electric traction featured Metropolitan-Vickers Bo-Bo 12 *Sarah Siddons* from 1922 - the UK's oldest operational electric locomotive, beautifully restored in maroon Metropolitan Railway livery. Modern electrics included Class 91 examples 91101 *Flying Scotsman* and 91110 *Battle of Britain Memorial Flight* from LNER's East Coast Main Line fleet.

In between eras, there was space for Classes 83, 85, 86, 87 and 89.

The innovative Class 93 tri-mode locomotive 93001 made its public debut, demonstrating Stadler Rail's cutting-edge technology combining 25kV electric, diesel and battery power in a single locomotive. Technical presentations throughout the weekend explained how this versatile machine represents the future of flexible freight haulage.

The event showcased Britain's continuing railway industry through modern rolling stock examples. Class 345 'Aventra' units, built at the host site for London's Elizabeth Line, demonstrated Derby's ongoing role in train construction.

Eurostar power car 3999 made a rare public appearance, representing Britain's connection to European high-speed rail networks.

The hydrogen-powered HydroFLEX train from Porterbrook offered visitors tours of its innovative hydrogen chamber, demonstrating future sustainable technologies. Engineers were on hand to explain how hydrogen fuel cells could revolutionize rail transport on non-electrified routes.

An InterCity 125 High Speed Train, comprising power cars 43159 *Rio Warrior* - the world's fastest diesel - and 43060,

Feeling blue… Class 58 58023 *Leicester Depot* meets brand-new GB Railfreight Class 99 99001.
MIKE WILD.

The Greatest Gathering offered unprecedented access to working railway facilities in recent years."

highlighted Derby's role in building their matching Mark 3 carriages that revolutionised BR's express services.

OPEN ACCESS

The Greatest Gathering offered unprecedented access to working railway facilities in recent years. Visitors could ride along Alstom's one mile test track in a Class 345 'Aventra' unit, normally serving Elizabeth Line passengers. The test facility, commissioned in 1999, allows trains to reach 40mph while testing various signalling and power supply systems.

The Train Zero facility provided insights into modern train testing, featuring static test rigs for software verification across Alstom's 'Aventra' fleet. Engineers demonstrated how virtual testing environments allow them to simulate years of operational conditions before trains enter service.

Guided tours of the production facilities revealed the sophisticated manufacturing processes behind modern trains. Visitors witnessed the assembly of bodyshells, the installation of complex electrical systems, and the final fitting-out stages where bare metal structures are transformed into passenger stock.

The STEM Hub provided interactive experiences designed to inspire future railway professionals. Against the backdrop of historic and modern exhibits, visitors explored railway technology through hands-on activities, driving simulators and virtual reality experiences. Young visitors could operate miniature signalling systems, understand the principles of electric traction, and learn about sustainable transport solutions. The Railway Challenge showcased locomotives built by university teams, with Derby and Sheffield entries operating passenger rides on specially laid track.

The turntable demonstrations, operating every half hour throughout each day, saw the Webb 'Coal Tank' spun around… dozens of times by the close of the weekend.

MODEL VILLAGE

The Model Railway Village, in association with Key Model World, occupied D Shop, housing over 30 layouts representing the finest in British railway modelling. This section deserved particular attention for *Hornby Magazine* readers.

Pete Waterman's Making Tracks dominated the village with his spectacular 64ft-long representation of Milton Keynes Central station in 'OO' gauge. The layout is part of his world record-breaking 208ft 'longest portable model railway' certified by Guinness World Records in April 2024. Waterman himself was present throughout the weekend, sharing anecdotes with the crowds.

TOP LEFT: There was even live steam inside the Works, such as this splendid weathered 5in gauge '4F'. NICK BRODRICK.
TOP RIGHT: Railwayana collector Richard Allen shows some of his – and others' – collection in G Shop. NICK BRODRICK.
CENTRE: A contrast in nose ends: 'Clayton' D8568 and 'Deltic' D9015 *Tulyar*. NICK BRODRICK.
ABOVE: Home! Midland Compound 1000. NICK BRODRICK.

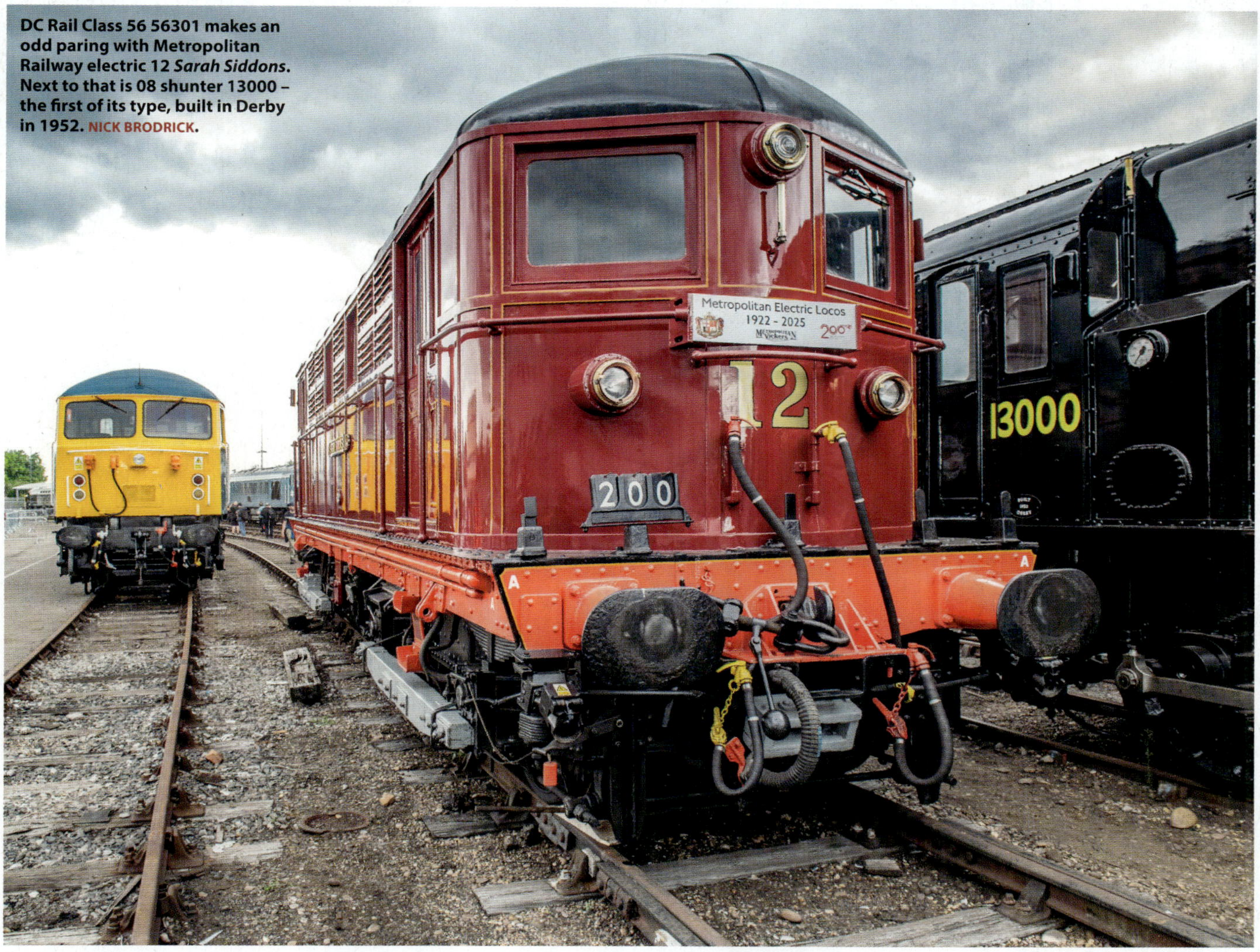

DC Rail Class 56 56301 makes an odd paring with Metropolitan Railway electric 12 *Sarah Siddons*. Next to that is 08 shunter 13000 – the first of its type, built in Derby in 1952. NICK BRODRICK.

'Peak', 'Shed', 'Warship'. MIKE WILD.

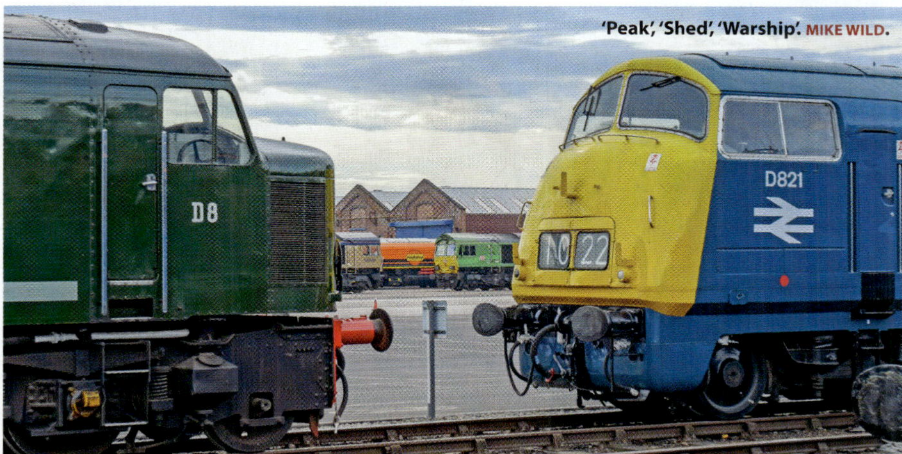

Key Model World debuted its brand-new Derby Litchurch Lane Works layout, modelling part of the host site using exclusive laser-cut building kits created by PJM Models. The 13ft x 2ft OO gauge scenes features an eight-track-wide works 'northlight' building with track set into 'concrete' panels, a second works building and gantry crane. This layout had been featured in *Hornby Magazine*'s July-September 2025 issues.

Twelve Trees Junction, the team's 24ft x 10ft Southern Region layout, made one of its last appearances in its current form(!), showcasing the final years of steam in the south London suburbs when it shared space with third-rail EMUs. ■

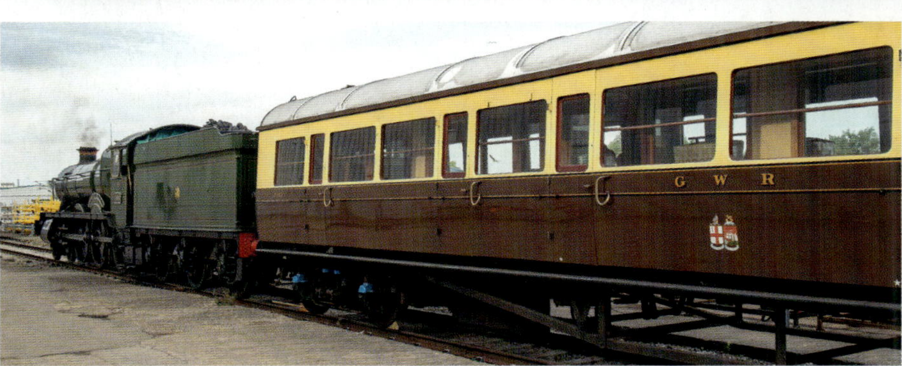

As well as locomotives, there were a selection of historic carriages. The Severn Valley's *Hagley Hall* is paired with GWR livery Collett stock. NICK BRODRICK.

DIGITAL SOUVENIR

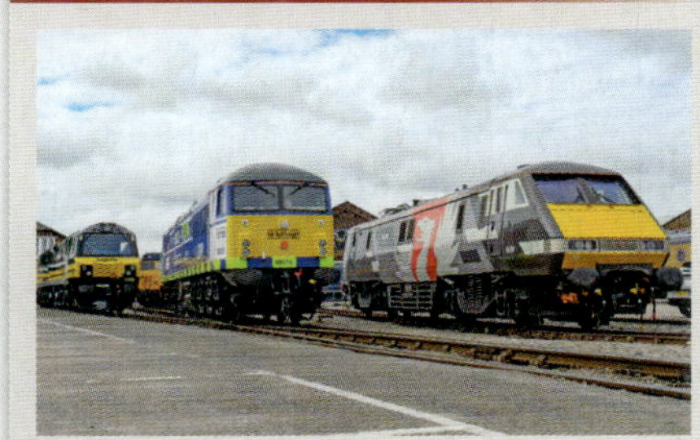

We've teamed up with Alstom to present a free digital download of the event guide at ***www.keymodelworld.com***

Exclusive products | Modelling essentials | Limited edition

KEY Publishing Model World SHOP

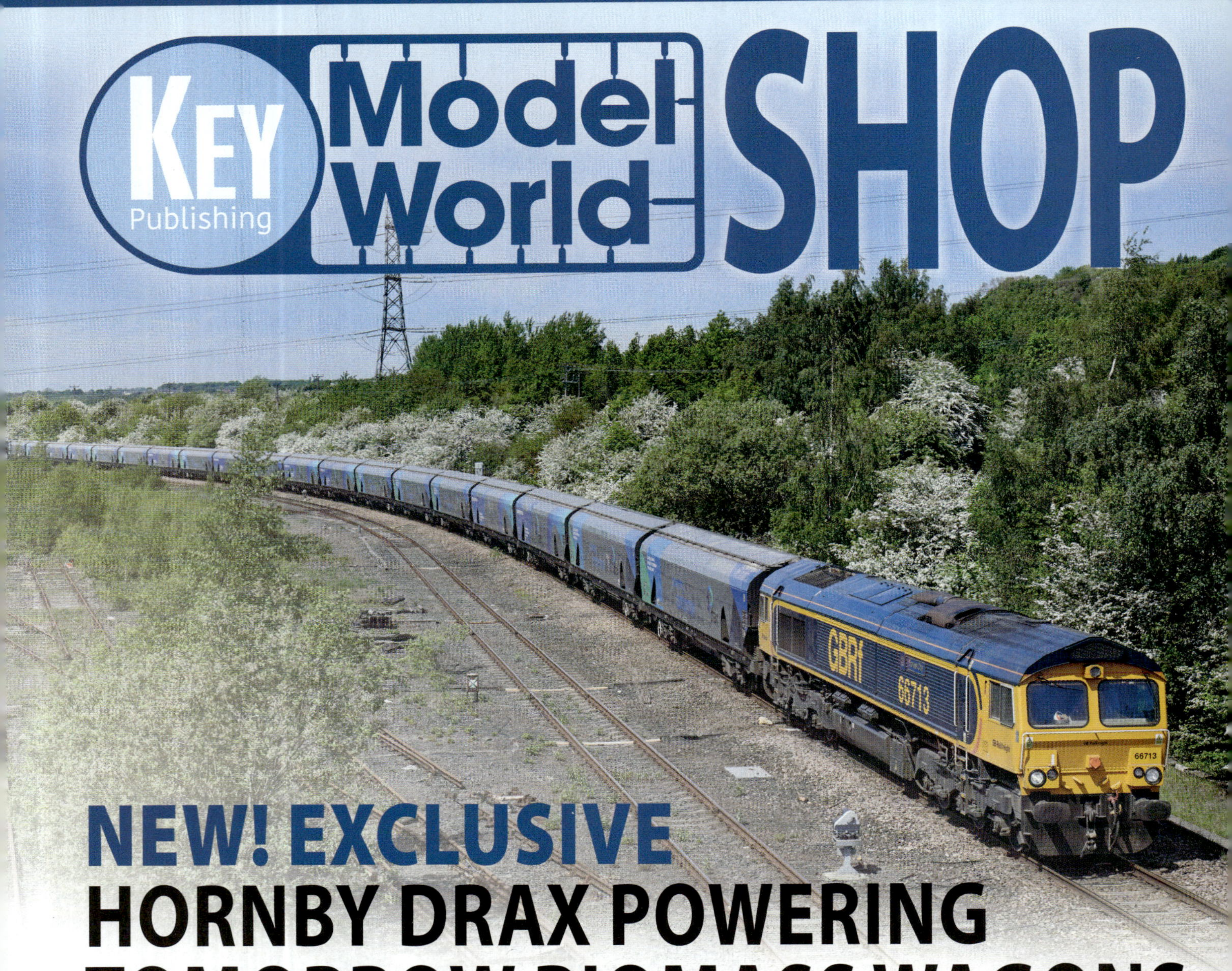

NEW! EXCLUSIVE

HORNBY DRAX POWERING TOMORROW BIOMASS WAGONS

Pre-order today for delivery in Spring 2026

Key Publishing has commissioned Hornby to produce a series of four unique twin packs modelling the Drax IIA-D biomass wagons in original Drax Powering Tomorrow livery. Each twin pack will feature individually numbered wagons allowing eight different IIA-Ds to be coupled together.

Pre-order today with a non-refundable £10 deposit per twin pack. Delivery expected Spring 2026.

FULL PRICE: £89.99 per twin pack

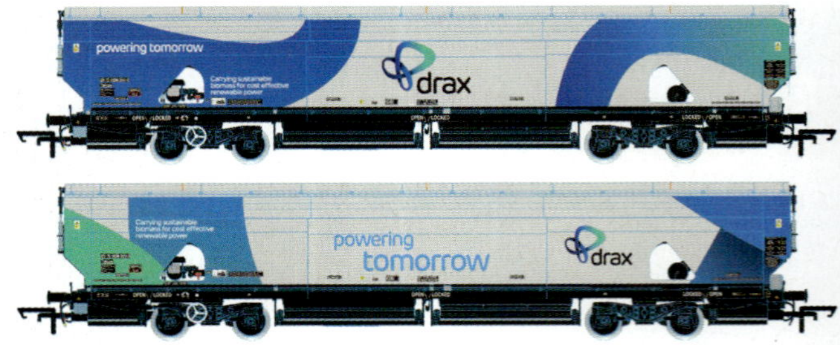

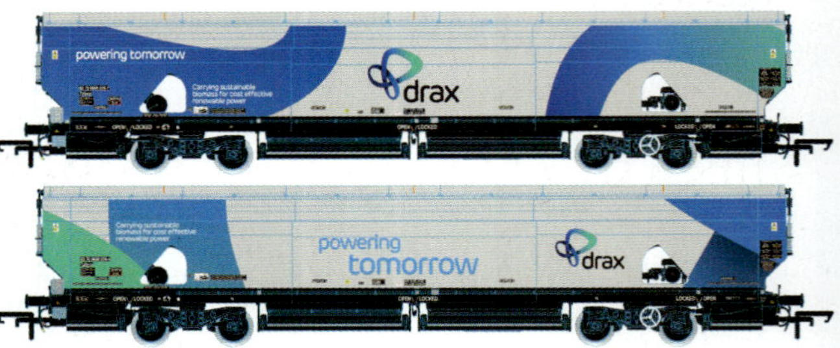

NEW! PRE-ORDER NOW - CLASS 60 60040 IN DB SCHENKER RED

Exclusive 'OO' gauge Accurascale Class 60 Territorial Army Centenary

FULL PRICE: • **£169.99** DCC ready • **£269.99** DCC sound fitted
Order now to secure yours with a £30 non-refundable deposit

PRE-ORDER NOW - LMR 'WD' 600 *GORDON*

Clark Railworks Special Edition 'WD' 2-10-0 in 1960s condition

FULL PRICE:
• **£295.00** DCC ready
• **£425.00** DCC sound fitted

Order now to secure yours with a £30 non-refundable deposit

PRE-ORDER NOW COLAS RAIL 43277 AND 43257

Exclusive 'OO' gauge Hornby HST train pack featuring Colas Rail HST power cars

FULL PRICE: • **£394.99** DCC ready • **£449.99** DCC sound fitted
Order now to secure yours with a £30 non-refundable deposit

PRE-ORDER NOW 56103 IN DCRAIL GREY

Exclusive Cavalex Models modern-era Class 56

FULL PRICE: • **£189.95** DCC ready • **£289.95** DCC sound fitted
Order now to secure yours with a £30 non-refundable deposit

LAST FEW - IN STOCK NOW!

Exclusive Hornby CrossCountry HST Farewell pack

FULL PRICE: • **£359.99** DCC ready • **£399.99** DCC sound fitted

IN STOCK NOW! - 47817 FOR 'OO'

Exclusive Heljan 'OO' gauge model of Porterbrook's Class 47

FULL PRICE: • **£199.95** DCC ready • **£299.95** DCC sound fitted

IN STOCK NOW! BACHMANN CLASS 40 40145

Add a unique railtour locomotive to your fleet for 'OO' gauge

FULL PRICE: • **£195.95** DCC ready • **£295.95** DCC sound fitted
NEW! Legomanbiffo sound fitted models **£299.95**

DUE NOVEMBER - CLASS 66 66794

Exclusive Accurascale 'OO' gauge Class 66 arriving soon

SOLD OUT ON PRE-ORDER - REGISTER YOUR INTEREST FOR REMAINING STOCK

CHECK OUT OUR FULL COLLECTION OF EXCLUSIVE MODELS HERE:

keymodelworld.com/shop

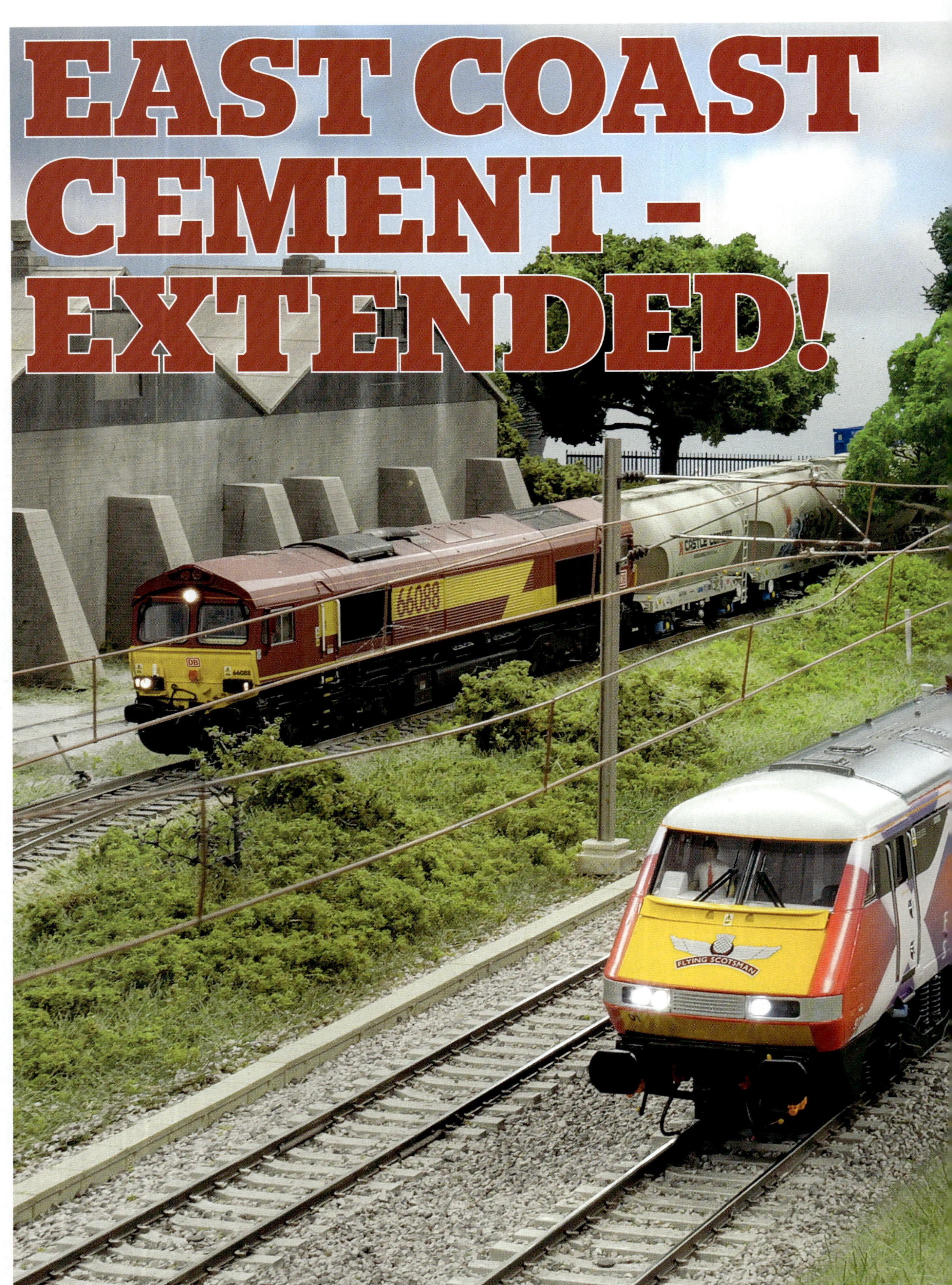

EAST COAST CEMENT – EXTENDED!

With just six weeks to go until the 2025 Great Electric Train Show the Hornby Magazine team decided to create a brand-new extension to East Coast Cement to introduce new features to the layout. **MIKE WILD** explains why it was built and how it has transformed the layout's operation. Photography, Mike Wild.

Looking through from the original layout into the new station scene, Class 91 91101 *Flying Scotsman* races north with a rake of Mk 4s as an HST departs in the background heading south. On the left 66088 eases into the cement works with a rake of PCA wagons.

STATISTICS

Layout name: East Coast Cement	
Length: 32ft	
Width: 10ft	
Gauge: 'OO', 16.5mm	
Period: 2015-2025, ECML	
Control: DCC, Roco Z21	

At the south end of the station a new Bachmann Class 350/4, 350407, draws away from a station stop with the new station behind. In the distance the original cement works can be seen.

It might sound a strange statement, but East Coast Cement had become too small. We'd changed its theme to West Coast Main Line to East Coast Main Line and at the same time the time period had moved forward to 2015-2025 bringing with it changes in traction and rolling stock that didn't really lend themselves to a 20ft long layout anymore.

Modern trains are long, and particularly container trains, and we were finding that the near 18ft length of the longest formation just didn't look right when it filled the entire scenic frontage. We are fortunate that this layout is an exhibition only scene, as that means we don't have to worry to much about where it fits, and this set the thought process moving forward about what we could do with the layout if it were to become longer.

For some time we've been talking about creating a new frontage for the 20ft storage yard which links to East Coast Cement, but in reality we weren't quite ready for a completely new project like that. It was first built in 2018 for Hornby Magazine Yearbook No. 11 at which time we had a 1995-2005 early privatisation West Coast Main Line theme to the layout which we had since moved away from to give the scene a new lease of life.

Having considered the options and also what we could do for display at the 2025 Great Electric Train Show adding 12ft to the original layout to introduce a station scene seemed like a logical and simple step – and one which, on paper, would be possible to complete in the six weeks prior to the show on October 11/12 at the Arena MK in Milton Keynes.

One of the primary aims was that we gave space to the full-length trains running on the

A new feature for East Coast Cement is a set of aggregate loading sidings alongside the line to and from the cement works. Cavalex Models Class 60 60029 *Ben Nevis* waits for its rake of JNA-T box wagons to be loaded as 66088 eases back along the line from the cement works after dropping off a rake of empty PCA tanks.

at an angle to the front of the layout, we had to introduce a second slight curve in the main line to take it across the new boards to join with the original tracks at the crossing. This ended up being quite simple to achieve, but before starting we did even consider building an entirely new end board, but that wouldn't have been possible in the time available.

The new 12ft section was originally planned to be quite simple. A through station with two platform faces was envisaged with a simple track running straight through behind to reach the cement works, possibly with an additional siding. However, on starting the build we soon realised there was much more potential available within the space available so the station grew to feature a bay platform at the rear while beyond that the line through to the cement works was joined by a pair of sidings to serve an aggregate loading point where rakes of JNA-T wagons could be staged for loading by excavators, much as they are at loading points around the country.

All this added up to a much more exciting scene and one which we could see would also introduce much greater operation to East Coast Cement – something which we felt was lacking from the original design which was essentially a double track main line round the outside with a cement works tucked inside.

The trackplan was redrawn on the fly as we started mocking up the layout with a trailing crossover being added on the main line to allow trains to arrive in the bay platform from the inner main line and then reverse back out onto the outer main line via the crossover after terminating at the station. There were also new points added to the aggregate sidings while the new functionality at the front had an impact on the storage yard at the rear which now needed a crossover for the bay platform shuttle and a second one to assist in managing train movements around the cement and aggregate operations.

We now had a huge job list to undertake to get the layout ready for the Great Electric Train Show, so it was very much a case of

layout. We wanted to see a Class 91 and eight Mk 4s with a DVT at the end sweeping through the scene and passing a full length HST set running the other way while freight activity continued in the yard behind. And there was also a need to create more space for the freight operation, as they were quite restricted by the position of the level crossing when it came to shunting movements from the cement works.

DIVISION
Having decided an extension was the way forward we needed a way of adding in new

length to the layout without needing radical changes to the original. There was an obvious point where new boards could be inserted, but there was a challenge to make the track formation work. Essentially the end board with the level crossing on it would be moved 12ft away from the end of the cement works allowing the new scene to be inserted in between. This in turn moved the level crossing more than a train length away from the cement works to facilitate more realistic operation.

However, with the tracks approaching the original baseboard joint next to the crossing

CrossCountry HST power car 43184 *Laira Diesel Depot* leads a Penzance-Newcastle working through the station with 43366 HST40 at the rear. This pair of power cars are exclusive Hornby Limited Editions made for Key Publishing.

dividing up the jobs to get it moving on multiple fronts at the same time. Mike took on the track laying and wiring while Mark and Ben built the platforms. Meanwhile in the background PJM Models Phil Moreton was working on bespoke signals for the layout as well as brand-new fencing for the station and cutting of a set of laser-cut cantilever overhead gantries for use in the station. It was all hands to the pump to get the build on the move.

DEADLINE

There's nothing quite like a deadline to focus you and that's exactly what drove the build of East Coast Cement's extension. We quickly had the track laid and the platforms built between us within one working day and that meant we could at least test that it would work and link to the original layout. However, now the hard part began as each part of the process had to be completed on time to allow the next to begin.

The most important next step was painting of the platforms as only once they were done could we move to add the ballast and start installing the overhead catenary through the station. The platforms we had chosen for this build were the concrete lintel design produced by PJM Models for Key Publishing. These offer choices for their finish with the standard kit have the lintels design included, but there is also an optional add on pack of scaffolding supports which were added under

The original layout is firmly part of the scene. A Hornby TransPennine Express Class 802 rounds the curve under the motorway bridge and passes an engineering train in the charge of a pair of Class 66s.

Looking across the platforms Cavalex Models Class 56 56049 has charge of an engineering working as a Dapol Class 68 arrives with a set of Accurascale Mk 5 coaches. In the background a Bachmann Class 150/2 waits in the bay platform.

two sections to add more detail and interest to the scene.

The painting was completed using a combination of aerosol spray cans and brush painting with the main surface being finished with Railmatch Roof Dirt (Cat No. 1406) and the outer stones with Ford Dove Grey. The brick detail underneath the concrete lintel platforms was picked out using Lifecolor Worn Brick (UA737) and Old Tile (UA740) dry brushed over the brick surface for a realistic finish.

As soon as the platforms were fully finished the overhead masts were installed so that we could check that the contact wires fitted as planned after which they were removed to make way for ballasting of the entire scene.

There was still another job to complete before then though as we wanted to add the lineside equipment which is so prevalent on the modern railway. Concrete cable troughs from West Hill Wagon Works were laid along the length of the new scene together with

Rusty Rails Modelling lineside cabinets and point heaters, axle counters and even cables linking the boxes together to bring the scene to life. We also prepared for the signals by positioning cabinets next to their locations.

With all this complete the big job of ballasting the entire 12ft scene was tackled across an afternoon at the end of a week meaning that the layout could be left alone to dry out thoroughly over the weekend ready for the next work session on the Monday.

A Hornby LNER Azuma thunders through the station non-stop as it passes the Network Rail compound (left) and one of the newly installed signals. Behind Accurascale Class 66 66167 heads a cement working destined for the cement works.

We were now at the beginning of the final detailing as we built up the landscape, added ground cover and moved onto lineside signage, platform furniture, platform fencing and the final details and weathering around the aggregate sidings to bring the scene to life. It was an intense process above the boards, but there was also lots happening beneath as Phil and Ben got everything set up for installation of the working signals as well as the new servo point motors which would control all the point operation.

There was another big task which we had to complete to match the front – a 12ft extension of the storage yard. That involved restoring three baseboards from old stored projects to useable condition and then laying 44 yards of track, four points, 66 copper clad sleepers, over 70 wire droppers to the tracks and all the new power bus underneath to take the main track feed to its distribution point. All of this was done in less than eight hours.

OPERATION

Changing the way East Coast Cement operated was high on the priority list. We'd always enjoyed taking the layout out to shows in its original form, but equally we knew it lacked a little in the operational interest both from our point of view and the public watching.

The length of the layout was a big part of this, but second and virtually equal was that trains didn't really have to do anything – we could just sequence them out of the storage, send them through the scenic section and bring them back with very little interaction on the main line. Most of the operational part came from the cement works, but even

The DMU shuttle from the bay platform adds greatly to the operational variety on the layout. It has a dedicated crossover in the storage yard at the rear allowing it travel back and forth from the bay on the correct line.

that was really limited by the length of the headshunt which crossed the level crossing within 2ft of leaving the sidings.

The extension with the station meant we now had reason to operate a greater variety of trains and that selected trains could stop at the station. The DMU bay platform shuttle was another great addition which really added

to the interest as it had to fit around the main line train operations and, with the right consideration, could be 'stolen' by the cement works operator to bring it back to the storage yard in between main line trains. The second crossover in the storage yard made it simple to operate too and is something we are looking at introducing into other layout plans.

An LNER HST passes through the station with 43305 leading. The overhead electrification masts are PJM Models laser-cut cantilever gantries which are designed to support handmade brass registration arms to hold the contact wires.

As the cement works was originally part of a layout called Shortley Bridge and Felton Cement Works we decided to revive the Shortley Bridge name for the new station. Signage is from Sankey Scenics.

Northern Rail signage by Sankey Scenics completes the platforms while a brand-new 3D printed platform fencing by PJM Models contains the passengers.

The Northern Rail Class 150 departs Shortley Bridge and passes the Network Rail compound as it crosses over onto the fast lines.

The freight operation was also massively improved as the headshunt space available to the cement section now meant the entire 22 wagon PCA rake could be brought out in one if needed without interfering with the level crossing while the aggregates sidings provide visual and operational interest at the rear of the station.

Extending the operation further was both the choice of operating system and the introduction of servo operated points together with fully functioning signals which automatically returned to red once a train had passed. The latter was managed via current detection with trains passing over a selected section of track triggering the signal to change meaning that driver's now needed to be aware of the signal aspect as to how they drove their train.

The servo point motors introduced a new level of reliability to the scenic section and saw the entire scene upgraded to the new motor type in place of the old solenoids which had served the cement works and main line from the layout's original construction in 2018.

Previously Gaugemaster Prodigy handsets had been used to operate the layout, but with an increasing number of trains and complex routes through the storage yard it needed a rethink. Following our experience with the Roco Z21 on Twelve Trees Junction that rethink didn't take long as it was instant choice to switch to the tablet control system which offers a full track diagram as well as easy to view locomotive rosters meaning that anyone can step into the driving seat following a short set of instructions on how to use the tablets. It just takes a bit of time to get used to the trackplan!

One of the advantages that with the Roco Z21 is that we can also now offer the opportunity for exhibition visitors to drive the layout. We had planned to do this at the Great Electric Train Show, but with a few teething troubles and final adjustments being needed as well as bedding in the new extension this wasn't quite as easy to achieve as we had hoped. Having completed the first show with the layout we can certainly see this being possible at future events when we take East Coast Cement out again.

FUTURE

What's next? Well there's still more we would like to do to the station scene including adding figures to the platform, adding power to the station lights as well as illuminating the buildings. The aggregates yard would benefit from further detailing too and potentially some lighting to go with the station to make the whole scene more complete.

There are other plans in the background too which might involve making the scenic area wider to introduce more features beyond the railway, but at this moment that's still on the drawing board.

The result of East Coast Cement's extension is even better than we had originally planned. The new operation and longer layout have made it so much more enjoyable to operate while the Roco Z21 control system makes it a joy to drive. Look out for more news on its next outings in future issues of *Hornby Magazine*. ∎

• *Our thanks to TMC, PJM Models, Sankey Scenics, DCC Concepts, Rusty Rails Modelling and West Hill Wagon Works in supporting the project to extend East Coast Cement.*

Farewell Somerset & Dorset… Bulleid 'Light Pacifics' 34006 *Bude* and 34057 *Biggin Hill* leave Chilcompton heading to Bath Green Park with the Locomotive Club of Great Britain's March 5 1966 railtour over the Mendips. The line closed to passengers the following day. **HIGH BALLANTYNE/RAIL PHOTOPRINTS.**

1966: WHEN BRITAIN'S RAILWAY CHANGED FOREVER

It was the year that branch line closures and the terminal decline of steam collided with the bright optimism of elecrtifcation. **NICK BRODRICK** looks back on the seismic events of 60 years ago.

For those who lived through 1966, the memories remain vivid: the smell of diesel fumes replacing coal smoke and hot oil, the sight of bulldozers tearing up century-old trackbeds, and the haunting silence where once steam whistles echoed.

This was the year mainland Britain's railways changed forever – a 12-month period of seismic transformation that saw beloved lines severed, steam banished from entire regions, yet paradoxically witnessed the continuous growth of the preservation movement that safeguards that heritage today.

England's World Cup victory, 'Swinging London', the Beatles at their creative peak contrasted sharply with the railway's retrenchment. While we celebrated modernity and cultural confidence, railways disappeared mile by mile.

Dr Richard Beeching's controversial *Reshaping of Britain's Railways* report had reached its devastating crescendo in 1964 when 1,058 miles of rail was culled. The following year saw another 600 miles wiped out. Some lines did remain as goods only branches, but that was cold comfort. Communities that had relied on

Plenty of smiling faces for BR chairman Dr Richard Beeching to the Bluebell Railway in April 1962 in the company of SECR 'P' 0-6-0T 323 *Bluebell*. He might not have been made quite as welcome after his report in 1963 that recommended the closure of thousands of miles of other branch lines. **ALAMY.**

Hello West Coast electrification. BR Class AL2 (82) E3051 hums at Manchester Piccadilly's bufferstops alongside 'Woodhead Electric' 27005 in October 1966. There's also a fleeting glimpse of a Class 305 EMU and spanking new Class 86 E3146. COLIN WHITFIELD/RAIL PHOTOPRINTS.

rail connections since Victorian times found themselves suddenly isolated from the railway map and would now have to rely on buses or privately owned cars.

The casualties read like a roll call of the fallen. On March 6 1966 the much-loved Somerset & Dorset Joint Railway breathed its last, ending 104 years of service across the Mendips. The so-called 'Slow and Dirty' had connected Bath with Bournemouth via a spectacular, if challenging, route – made especially famous thanks to the enterprising photography of Ivo Peters.

Perhaps even more shocking was the systematic dismemberment of the Great Central Railway. Sir Edward Watkin's grand vision of a railway to mainland Europe, built to continental loading gauge with gentle gradients and sweeping curves, fell victim to the accountant's pen. In September 1966, the Aylesbury – Rugby section closed to passengers, severing what had been Britain's last inter-city main line to be built before High Speed 1 opened many decades later.

To increase speed and punctuality on the Great Western Main Line, freshly rid of all steam, a small number of the South Wales-allocated English Electric Type 3s were re-geared for 100mph running, and tested on the Paddington - South Wales, Bristol and Exeter passenger services. Despite the accelerated timings, the benefits were not considered sufficient and the experiment faded into obscurity. In May 1966, Bo-Bos D6892 and D6879 growl out of Paddington as they pass Ranelagh Bridge fuel point with a smart rake of blue and grey Mk1s. RAIL PHOTOPRINTS.

The prestige *'Bournemouth Belle'* stands ready for departure to Waterloo in late 1966 behind the filthiest rebuilt Bulleid 'West Country' No. 34004 *Yeovil*, albeit still wearing its nameplate unlike many of its classmates. **ALAMY.**

The irony wasn't lost on observers – here was a modern engineered railway, built for speed and efficiency, being torn up even while lesser lines survived.

The enthusiast community responded to 1966's other upheavals with numerous commemorative railtours. These events, often bittersweet affairs, allowed final travels with threatened locomotive and unit types over similarly doomed routes.

Most poignant were the farewell tours over the Somerset & Dorset and Great Central lines; both featuring Bulleid 'Pacifics' as well as an eclectic mix of other power.

These closures formed part of Beeching's wider programme, targeting over 5,000 miles of track and 2,363 stations. The then British Railways chairman's report of three years earlier had set the agenda, only refined by the 1965 report *The Development of the Major Railway Trunk Routes*. His doctrine was simple: concentrate resources on profitable inter-city routes while eliminating duplicate and loss-making branches.

MARCH OF MODERNISATION

And so, 1966 wasn't solely about destruction as might be casually assumed, as BR pushed ahead with ambitious modernisation plans.

The new Euston station, opened to coincide with electrification of the West Coast Main Line was public symbol of this brave new world. Gone were the classical Doric arch and Great Hall, replaced by a modernist structure of glass and concrete which proclaimed efficiency rather than the forgotten legacy of the original London and Birmingham Railway.

It's July 1966, and while *Yeovil* is still in Southern Region service (top picture), another starts to rust at Barry Scrapyard. **ALAMY.**

Euston's Doric Arch would be demolished…

… In favour of a bold, bright new booking hall. **BOTH: ALAMY.**

The BR corporate image had also just received similar treatment. New signage appeared across the network, featuring the distinctive double-arrow logo and Rail Alphabet typeface designed by Jock Kinneir and Margaret Calvert. Station nameboards, timetables, and publicity material adopted a unified appearance, projecting the newly shortened British Rail in name as well as network. The nationalised railway wanted to be seen as a modern, integrated transport system rather than unnecessary regional fiefdoms, as it might have hitherto appeared.

BR's classic blue and grey had been introduced a couple of years earlier, but by 1966 was spreading fast in place of the muted steam-era colour palette.

Freight operations underwent radical transformation with the introduction of 'containerisation' and large Freightliner terminals. This revolution in goods handling, central to Beeching's vision, promised to make rail freight competitive with road haulage. The first purpose-built Freightliner terminals opened, equipped with massive gantry cranes capable of transferring containers between rail and road in minutes rather than the hours required for traditional wagon-load traffic.

THEY THINK IT'S ALL OVER

A poignant aspect for enthusiasts in 1966 was of course steam's accelerating demise.

The Western Region had already eliminated steam in 1965, but a few now alien GWR locomotives soldiered on into 1966, such as a clutch of '56XX' 0-6-2Ts at Croes Newydd shed, which had been taken over by the London Midland Region two years before.

Naturally, in steam's place came new diesel and electric locomotives, most notably the Class 86 electrics turned out from Doncaster Works and Vulcan Foundry in 1965/6 for West Coast Main Line duties. The arrival of the 100mph machines, delivering 3,600 horsepower, coincided with the most ambitious electrification programme in British railway history. For April 1966 marked a watershed with the inauguration of full electric services between Euston and Manchester Piccadilly. The completion of this section represented years of work installing overhead wires, upgrading signalling,

Asquith Xavier begins his new job as platform staff at Euston in August 1966 after his campaign to lift a ban on black workers at the station was successful. **ALAMY.**

Veteran Adams 'O2' 20 *Shanklin* climbs south from Sandown in late summer 1966, running to its namesake village. BR passenger steam on the island ended for good on December 31. **PETER ZABEK.**

A scene that epitomises the final run down for steam. Saltley shed's missing roof allows midsummer sunlight on its resting Stanier contingent, including '8Fs' 48214 and 44777. Days when it would be less tolerable for steam raisers and cleaners would soon be over anyway – the shed closed to steam in March 1967. BRIAN ROBBINS/RAIL PHOTOPRINTS.

and rebuilding stations. Stanier '8Fs' or BR Standard '4MT' 4-6-0s were often employed on wiring engineering trains.

Naturally, the 'leccy' programme didn't stop there. By December, electric trains served Coventry, Birmingham New Street, Walsall, Wolverhampton, and Stafford. Instead of the traditional DC system, 25kV AC overhead was adopted as standard after careful study of European practice. Only the northern section from Weaver Junction to Glasgow Central remained to complete the WCML's metamorphosis into the country's premier electric railway of the era.

This massive investment reflected both Beeching's second report recommendations and growing political recognition that Britain lagged behind continental neighbours in railway modernisation. The sight of overhead wires marching across the landscape became symbolic of progress, even as branch lines withered.

In private industry, it was the end of the construction line for Beyer, Peacock. A batch of BR Class 25/3s became the last locomotives to be constructed at the Manchester Works, which had been established in 1854 and became synonymous with supplying motive power all over the world.

POLITICAL WINDS OF CHANGE

Harold Wilson's Labour government, re-elected in March 1966, inherited the Beeching programme but gradually shifted emphasis. While closures continued, the concept of 'socially necessary' railways gained traction. Subsidies were introduced for loss-making but essential services, acknowledging that pure commercial criteria couldn't govern all transport decisions.

Brock troughs on the West Coast Main Line nod to the old age as 'Black Five' 45493 paces south with an Up fitted-goods in August 1966 as road traffic flows along the new M6. ALAMY.

This philosophical shift reflected growing unease about Beeching's harsh medicine. Rural communities protested vigorously about lost services, while urban areas faced increasing road congestion. The government's response, tentative in 1966, laid groundwork for future Passenger Transport Executives and integrated transport planning.

Labour's policies began recognising railways' social value beyond profit margins. Transport Minister Barbara Castle, appointed in December 1965, brought fresh thinking to the ministry, coinciding with Beeching's departure. While unable to halt the closure programme immediately, she initiated reviews that would eventually moderate its impact.

Amidst operational upheaval, 1966 witnessed significant social progress within British Rail.

The campaign by Asquith Xavier, a Dominica-born guard, against workplace discrimination achieved a landmark victory. In July, British Rail ended its colour bar policy at Euston station, where West Indian staff had been prevented from working in public-facing roles.

The Western Region's last official steam (standard gauge) locomotive of January 1966, 'Modified Hall' 6998 *Burton Agnes Hall*, is now preserved at Didcot Railway Centre, together with another late survivor – 'Large Prairie' 6016 (withdrawn December 1965). ALAMY.

Standard gauge steam on BR was on a very short leash, but industry would keep the tradition going for another couple of decades. S&L Minerals' Pen shed in Corby hosts its pair of Robert Stephenson & Hawthorn 'Uglies' 57 and 64 sometime in 1966. **J. B. DODD/RAIL PHOTOPRINTS.**

Xavier's stand against institutional racism, supported by his union and progressive politicians, forced British Rail to confront discriminatory practices. The victory at Euston rippled across the network, contributing to broader changes in employment practices.

PRESERVATION'S EARLY CHAMPIONS

As 1966 ended, the preservation movement's pioneers could reflect on remarkable achievements against overwhelming odds. The Bluebell, Ffestiniog, and Middleton and Talyllyn railways had already proved narrow-gauge and branch line preservation possible on railways closed 'before Beeching'.

The later mass preservation movement, much of which born from 1966's multiple traumas, would eventually operate more railway mileage than the doctor closed. Heritage railways would employ thousands, attract millions of visitors, and contribute significantly to local economies. The irony wasn't lost – lines closed as uneconomic in 1966 would thrive as tourist attractions by century's end.

The Isle of Wight's transition from steam on December 31 1966 to elderly London Underground stock prompted the Wight Locomotive Society's formation. Recognising the uniqueness of the island's railway heritage, preservationists secured locomotives and stock, laying foundations for today's successful Isle of Wight Steam Railway (see separate feature).

December brought another significant development with the Corris Railway Society's establishment. This narrow-gauge line in west Wales, a figurative stone's throw from the Talyllyn, had closed in 1948, but enthusiasts refused to let it die. Their determination to reopen sections of the railway would ultimately bear fruit, with 1.5 miles now restored between Maespoeth Junction and Corris, operated by replicas of the original 'Tattoo' and 'Falcon' saddle tanks.

As well as the smaller machines of the private lines, a collective of entrepreneurs had the pluck to save express locomotives too. Western Region 'Castle' 7029 *Clun Castle* was bought by businessman Patrick Whitehouse, while LNER 'A4' 60009 *Union of South Africa* was saved by farmer John Cameron.

Adding a splash of colour to the muted steam liveries was Alan Pegler's Apple Green 'A3' 4472 *Flying Scotsman*, which was a regular performer on railtours from north of the border to south of the Thames.

Dai Woodham's Barry scrapyard was already becoming a mecca for preservationists, providing temporary reprieve for hundreds of condemned locomotives. That the South Wales yard was destined to become an unlikely source of more than 200 locomotives for preservation was still to be discovered.

BEECHING'S LEGACY

By December 1966, many of Beeching's 1963 recommendations had been implemented. Most branch lines earmarked for closure were gone or scheduled for imminent withdrawal. Investment concentrated on trunk routes – the West Coast, East Coast, and Great Western main lines received priority for modernisation. Electrification continued to spread across the Southern Reagion, which would be totally devoid of steam by summer 1967.

Yet cracks appeared in the Beeching orthodoxy. Closed lines didn't always generate predicted road traffic patterns. Some communities found themselves isolated without adequate bus replacements. The environmental and social costs of wholesale closures became apparent, contributing to the further political shift towards subsidised operation of socially necessary services.

The containerisation revolution, while technically successful, couldn't stem freight's drift to road transport; Freightliner services operated well but captured less traffic than projected. Traditional wagon-load freight, the railways bread and butter for over a century, waned as customers switched to door-to-door road haulage.

As 1966 drew to its close, the network was barely two-thirds its 1960 size. Steam traction, apart from isolated pockets in the south, North West and North East, had vanished.

Yet something deeper was lost. The railway's role as universal service provider, reaching every market town and rural valley, had ended. The intimate connection between communities and their stations, goods yards, and signal boxes was severed. Branch line individualism gave way to corporate uniformity.

The British railway emerged smaller but more focused, modern but less comprehensive. The preservation movement, 1966's unexpected heritage legacy, ensures future generations can experience what might have been almost totally wiped out. ∎

MOVING MOUNTAINS
BR BRUSH TYPE 5/CLASS 60 DIESEL ELECTRIC LOCOMOTIVE
RUN 2
1:76.2 SCALE / OO GAUGE

DC/DCC READY
£169.99

DCC SOUND
£269.99

New liveries of the ultimate Class 60 join the Accurascale line-up! Our heavy 'Tug' weighs in at over 800g, comes with assured all-wheel drive and a powerful five pole skew-wound motor, so it can live up to the reputation of the real thing. With sophisticated lighting modes, Accurathrash speakers, 'powerbank' and designed from scans of the real thing, as well as information from the people who built them, it's a blockbuster model. To add to your fleet **pre-order** direct from **accurascale.com**, or at your local stockist from £169.99. Realistic models at Realistic prices.

Pre-production samples subject to change

All Class 60 models feature

- High level of detail
- Die-cast chassis
- Five-pole motor with twin flywheels
- DCC ready & DCC sound (ESU loksound v5) options
- Details specific to individual prototypes
- High fidelity metal and plastic parts
- Sprung metal buffers
- Helical gears for maximum performance
- PowerBank line of capacitors
- Comprehensive lighting functions
- A lifetime warranty
- And other typical Accurascale features

Scan the QR Code or visit: www.accurascale.co.uk to view the full range of Class 60 locomotives currently available to order.

190+ STANDS!

- **Model railways** • **Scale modelling**
- **Radio control** • **Demonstrations**
- **Interactive exhibits** • **Slot cars**

DISCOUNT ADVANCE TICKETS BOOK NOW AND SAVE!

Offering early entry from 9.30am each day

- **Adults** £20.00 *(subscriber £18.00)* • **Weekend** £40.00
- **Children** £10.00 • **VIP** ticket £60.00 *(limited availability)*

information and updates:

modelworldlive

976/25

Masterpieces in the
GALLERY

From scenic majesty to urban grot, the standard of layouts to appear in the pages of *Hornby Magazine* never ceases to amaze as this selection from the past year will testify.

Feel the autumn chill on the back of your neck in the Cumbrian mountains as a DMU calls at Horton. This stunning Settle – Carlisle Railway inspired scene is the 'N' gauge creation of Andrew McDonald. The 1960s-era layout featured in HM209. JONATHAN NEWTON.

Knaresborough Viaduct in Yorkshire ranks as one of Britain's most beautiful. Gresley 'D49' 4-4-0 62760 *The Cotswold* crosses the Harrogate Model Railway Group's 'OO' rendition, as featured in HM 212. JONATHAN NEWTON.

Lydgate is one of four individual 'OO' Western Region scenes joined together as one functioning layout by Ian Perrin. A BR Class 101 DMU arrives on the branch line as an NCB Sentinel 0-4-0VBT shunts the higher colliery sidings. This multi-level layout featured in HM 216. JONATHAN NEWTON.

'Britannia' 70006 *Robert Burns* is about to disappear beneath the South Downs having passed through Pettleworth Down station on Nick and James Wright's superb 'N' gauge model. See the full feature in HM 218. JONATHAN NEWTON.

It's the mid-1970s in the north of England as fictional Andrew Barclay 0-4-0ST *R & J Colliery No 1* shuffles open wagons around its namesake colliery. Built by Robbert Jan De Vries, it featured in HM 219. JONATHAN NEWTON.

ENGINE HOUSE

Bright autumn colours are a surprisingly rarely modelled season, but Terry Tew couldn't resist the setting his Great North of Scotland Railway Tellindalloch sometime in October- November. Caledonian Railway 'Jumbo' 0-6-0 57565 rolls into the branch line terminus, which featured in HM 220. JONATHAN NEWTON.

Glasgow Eastfield TMD – spread across 70ft x 40ft – is one of the most spectacular layouts to ever feature in *Hornby Magazine*. Mick Worrall's built this 'O' gauge BR era epic after the lockdown of 2020. See issue HM 215 for the full story. MIKE WILD

TELLINDALLOCH

The Southern Railway – Down Under!
Mike Scott's room-filling High Weald
inter-war layout is inspired by the
former 'Cuckoo Line'. 'King Arthur' 751
Etarre passes 'Atlantic' 2421 *South
Foreland*. This layout was featured
in HM 209. JONATHAN NEWTON .

The Yard combines 7mm:1ft standard gauge and narrow gauge in a small space. The team-built layout showcases a concentration of high-detail cranes and gantries, beneath which a 'Gronk' 0-6-0DM engages in a spot of shunting. See HM 210 for the full report. TREVOR JONES.

Slate meets coal: John Pinion and Emma Brown have exploited the array of splendid 'OO' and '009' offerings to create Priory Park. Andrew Barclay 0-4-0ST *Stonehaven* propels its 16 Ton mineral wagons off stage as George England 0-4-0STT *Prince* arrives with a string of loaded slate wagons. This compact two-tier layout featured in HM 218. JONATHAN NEWTON.

Is this the best indoor model ever made? Pendon Museum's Vale of the White Horse scene has been in development for decades; its 70th anniversary was marked in HM 206. PAUL ELLIS.

Transport for London clad 66721 *Harry Beck* rumbles over the Grand Union Canal near Croxley on Eric French's Metropolitan Line inspired layout Harefield Road, which was a focus of HM 221. JONATHAN NEWTON

WARWICK
AVENUE
MAIDA
BAKER
STREET
PORT
ST.
STRE
GOODGE
STREET
TOTTENHAM
COURT ROAD
OLBORN
(KINGSWAY)
MANSION
HOUSE
MONUME
PADDINGTON
REGENTS
PARK
CO ENT
DEN
EB Railfreight
London
Transport
Museum
Supports London Transport Museum
Harry Be
LAD
GROVE
FEC X
FELLOWS MORTON
& CO LTD
FERRET

THE DESTINATION FOR
RAIL MODELLING ENTHUSIASTS

Visit us today and discover all our latest releases

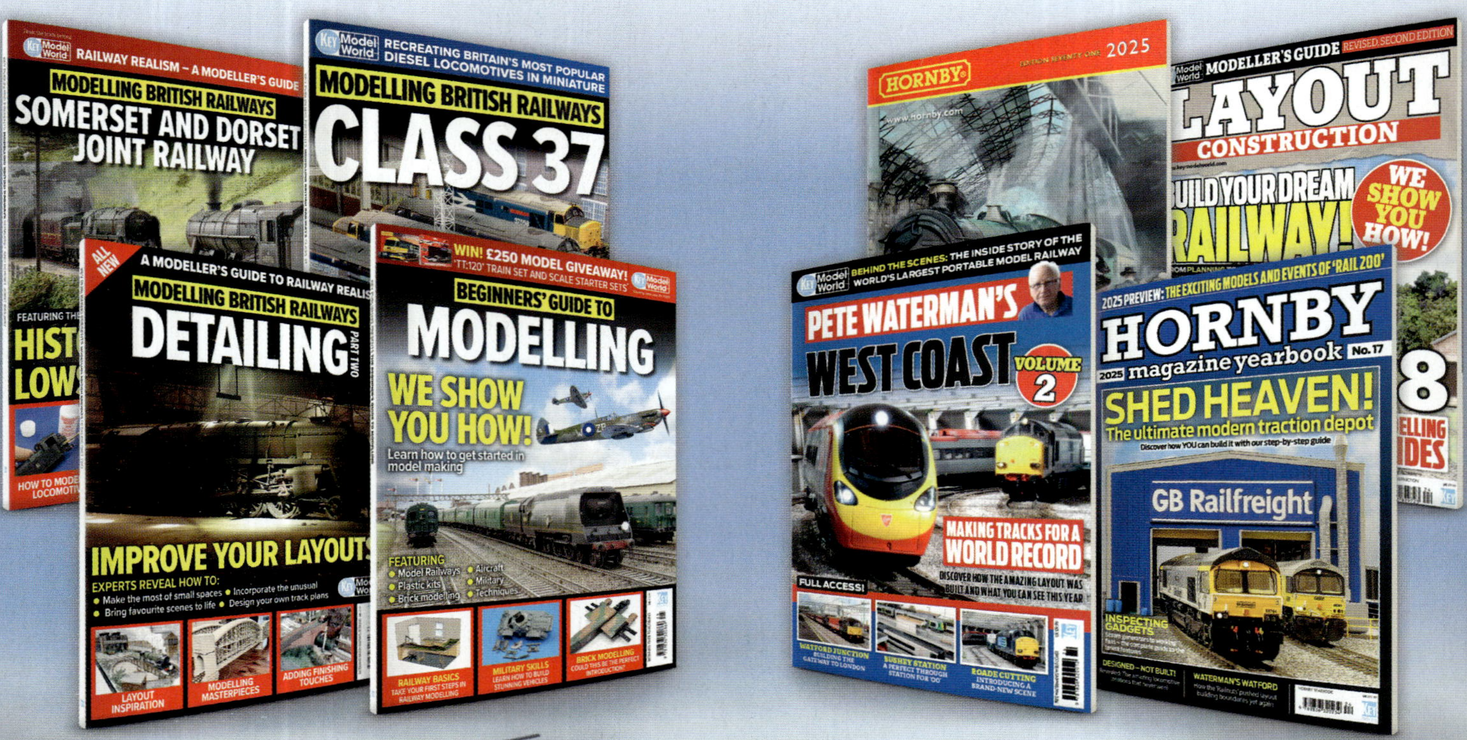

Order from our online shop today...

shop.keymodelworld.com/specials

Call +44 (0)1780 480404 *(Monday to Friday 9am - 5.30pm GMT)*

Free 2nd class P&P on BFPO orders. Overseas charges apply.

714/2

AN EVEN UGLIER DUCKLING!

You'll have heard of a Bulleid 'Q1', but what about his 'Q2'? **TREVOR JONES** reveals how he created a tank engine version of one of the Southern's ungainly goods engines.

The ultimate Bulleid kit-bash? The finished 'Q2' 0-6-4T 33050 *Tunbridge Wells* on shed at the outdoor Flackwell Heath. Salt was used for the temporary impression of snow, which will dissolve after the next rain shower. **TREVOR JONES.**

This is about as far as Bulleid's concept for a tank engine version of his 'Q1' ever got as part of the development work that ultimately led to the creation of the 0-6-6-0T 'Leader'. Even though the so-called 'Q2' was never built, original outline blueprints such as this provides plenty of inspiration for imaginative modelling. TREVOR JONES COLLECTION.

The original (and very much real) 'Q1' 0-6-0, represented by 33020 and 33027 between railtour duties at Chichester on 5 September 1965. Forty were built by the Southern Railway during the Second World War, featuring several cost and weight saving austerity features, like no running boards. **COLOUR RAIL.**

Something that little bit out of the ordinary often catches the eye when visiting an exhibition… Like a model of a locomotive that never existed!

I won't be alone to admit to having always been fixated by the myriad different locomotive designs through history, prototypical or otherwise. And yet I have never had a locomotive-that-never-was run on my 'OO' garden layout. Until now!

Even though manufacturers are producing ready-to-run types that we never dreamt would be available, we still haven't had a model of a class which was proposed but never built, unlike German modellers. Over this side of the Channel, we have a long history of 'what if?' liveries being applied to otherwise authentic prototypes.

But to achieve the truly fanciful, *yet plausible*, us Brits must take matters into our own hands.

When researching unusual, proposed designs from railway history, those of the Southern Railway's last Chief Mechanical Engineer Oliver Bulleid are among the very most varied and interesting.

I *could* have attempted a full scratch-built model, but while the mind is willing the fingers and eyes are struggling to work as they used to…

However, since the advent of 3D printing and the amazing possibilities it can readily realise, several of these proposed designs are appearing, some of which fit existing ready-to-run chassis.

I came across a Shapeways-marketed Bulleid 0-6-4T engine, which he had seemingly intended to base on the original 'Q1' 0-6-0. In fact, there were several versions proposed using different wheel arrangements. The design that interested me, and which I found a rough line drawing for, used the 'Q1' boiler, cylinders and driving wheels as a might-have-been 1940s replacement for London South Western Railway 'M7' 0-4-4Ts on branch line and suburban commuter steam services, as well as empty stock moves.

Naturally, a Hornby 'Q1' chassis is an essential part of this Frankenstein build, and I opted for a 'West Country'/'Battle of Britain' four-wheel leading truck to provide a donor rear bogie to make an 0-6-4 arrangement.

And with these parts in hand, I set to work.

CUT AND SHUT

First, the buffer beam and front section of the 3D-body moulding was cut away, as these are already present on the Hornby chassis. To fit the chassis at the right height meant grinding away some of the edge and similarly the inside of the roof of the 3D body.

At the front of the chassis is a threaded cylindrical part of the printing which lines up with the chimney. Without access to a shrink ray to climb inside the bodyshell makes measuring the space between the cylindrical nodule and the body shell impossible. However, I found a brass turned rod which had been threaded through at 8BA; this was attached with a sawn-off bolt to the chassis. Even so, I slightly underestimated the distance between the chassis and the underside of the chimney.

A 'Q1' tank engine… without the tanks! The sole surviving 'Charlie' No. C1 (BR 33001) is temporarily separated from its tender at the National Railway Museum in 2022, providing a good view of the spartan cab layout. **NICK BRODRICK.**

This was rectified by attaching a washer to the brass rod. I then found a bolt which had a large enough head to allow it to sit in the chimney recess and threaded it through the washer into the brass rod which I tapped to the appropriate thread for the bolt.

I had to cut a lump off the rear of the chassis to allow the rear bogie to be attached far enough forward for its wheels to clear the buffers. I then attached a brass bracket to this which almost aligned itself level with the underside of the cab; a plastic card spacer was glued to the underside of the cab and a bolt was secured to the top of the footplate passing through it and the Plasticard space.

In cutting off this rear section of the chassis I inadvertently skimmed the threaded printing which had held the electrical connection to the 'Q1's' tender. I managed to tap it with an 8BA thread and insert a sawn-off bolt, securing it with Araldite epoxy. I drilled out to a larger diameter the bogie linkage mounting hole so that it fitted over this tubular printing. I then found a large lumpy old washer which held the bogie linkage in place when locked with an 8BA nut.

The rear of the bogie had to have a section of metal ground away to allow the fixing of the coupling and for it not to protrude behind the locomotive. This was glued to the top of the bogie casting; on the underside an additional pickup was added by attaching it via a piece of copper paxilon insulating strip glued to the bogie. The leads from the motor that originally went through to the tender connection had to be extended to be able to be soldered to the paxilon strip.

A small piece of lead was glued to the top of the bogie to give it additional weight.

I also had to remove the resistor to enable it to clear the inside of the body.

PRINTED AND PRIMED

The next stage was to fit handrail knobs, whistle, water filler caps and steps up the rear of the bunker. These were all found in my bits-and-pieces box; the latter once part of a semaphore signal, bent and cut to fit. Lamp brackets were fitted from cut pieces of copper staple.

I primed the body with Halfords grey primer, but only after sanding as much as possible to remove the 3D printing lines. Because this model is made by the filament process, it leaves more marks than resin 3D castings which were a hitherto go-to for such conversion projects.

The next stage was to assemble the body and chassis to check there if loco and bogie successfully negotiated my tightest, 2ft 6in inner radius curve.

Trial running on my garden layout produced the result that my attachment performed perfectly, and the haulage capacity was more than adequate for the trains it had been designed to pull.

This accomplished, the chassis was separated from the body again. The body was sprayed gloss black and lined out with HMRS transfers. I chose the fictional number 33050, using the logic that it followed directly on from the 'Q1' class.

I therefore call this creation the class 'Q2'.

With the Southern and Bulleid's liking for named engines, I decided it would be named after commuter and branch line towns, plucking for *Tunbridge Wells*. I had nameplates and front number etched by Planet Industrials.

With these applied, the 0-6-4T was re-varnished. While still very slightly tacky, I liberally applied weathering powders onto all areas, apart the side tanks which just had a sprinkling.

'Q1' injector parts were acquired from South Eastern Finecast and with the addition of brass wire I cobbled together 'units' that look satisfactory.

This concoction was attached to a plastic square section by gluing to the insides of the body behind the cab steps and side tanks, inserting it into pre-drilled lugs. Together with the the injectors were hand painted and weathered by airbrush with the mechanism running.

So what next? Perhaps a Bulleid 2-8-2 should join the Great Wakering Whitefield & Flackwell Heath Railway… ■

Trevor Jones' unusual 0-6-4T makes for a striking comparison with its more conventional Southern Region six-coupled relative – Wainwright 0-6-0 'C' 31227. **TREVOR JONES.**

STEP-BY-STEP / CREATING A FRANKENSTEIN 'Q2'

An exploded view of the main constituent parts: Shapeways body, Hornby Q1 chassis, and Hornby 'Light Pacific' bogie.

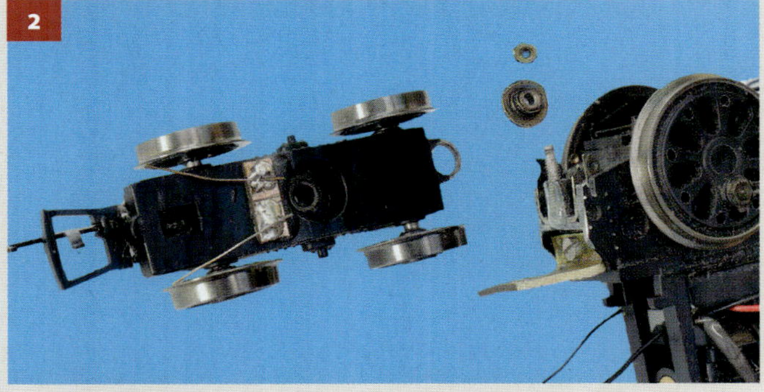

The bogie has had its mounting hole enlarged and the pickup affixed to the underside. The rear of the frames has been ground off and a bolt glued into the original tender tubular fixing. A brass bracket has been attached to the chassis to allow it to be attached to the underside of the cab floor.

The body now has had the front buffer beam assembly and rear buffers removed and the support for the rear of the chassis added under the cab floor. The chassis has had a section of the frames ground down to reduce the width, allowing the 3D body to fit. At the front, a brass cylinder and washer enables the print to be bolted in place through the chimney.

Prior to fitting the injectors 33050 was given a good run around the garden layout to ensure that the bogie rode well.

THE DESTINATION FOR
MODELLING ENTHUSIASTS
Visit us today and discover all our latest releases

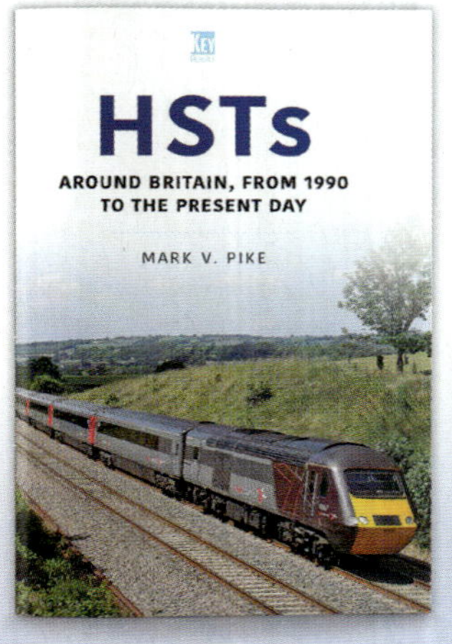

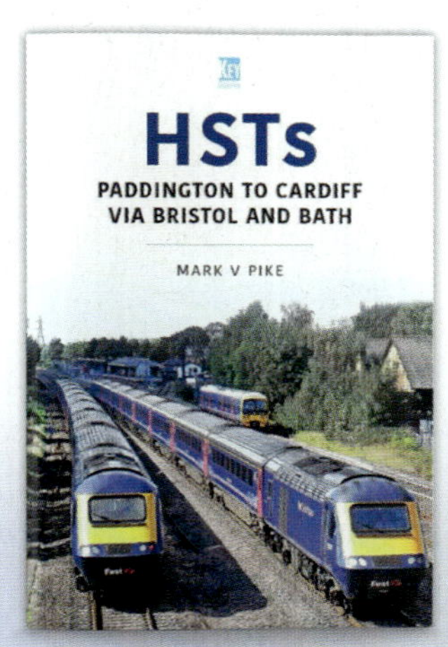

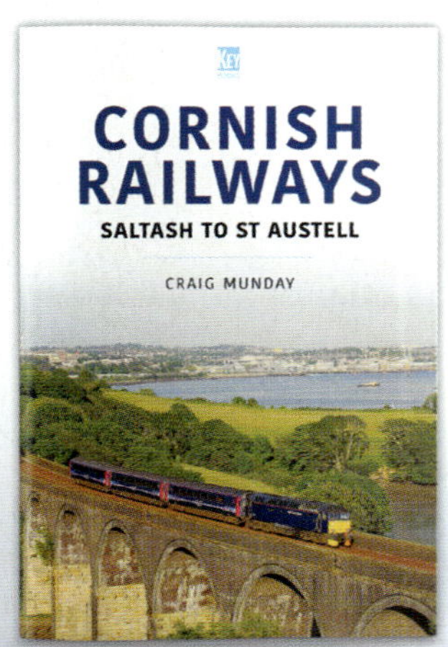

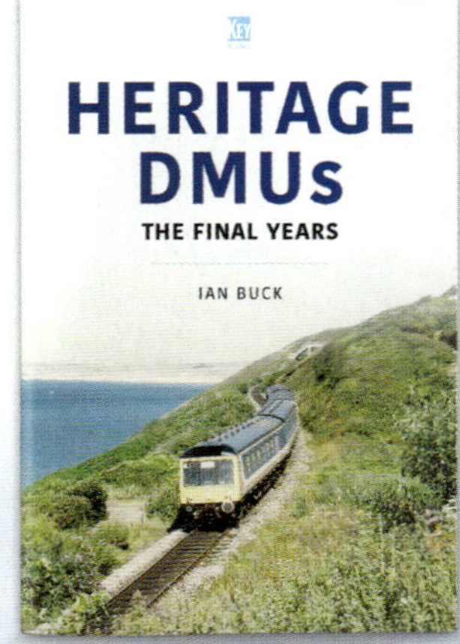

Order from our online shop...
keybooks.co.uk
Call +44 (0)1780 480404 *(Monday to Friday 9am - 5.30pm GMT)*
Free 2nd class P&P on BFPO orders. Overseas charges apply.

899/25

Maidenhead Bridge is one of the stunning symbols of Brunel's Main Line. Marking the 175th anniversary of the Great Western Railway, Castle 5043 *Earl of Mount Edgcumbe* speeds west over the River Thames in April 2011 running non-stop between Paddington and Bristol Temple Meads. PETER ZABEK.

FACT INTO FICTION

Few of us could ever fit a true scale prototype station into our homes in 4mm scale. Here, **PAUL LUNN** outlines how you can draw on inspiration from locations in the Thames Valley to design a space-saving layout with the vital elements of the real thing.

What's the best place to start when considering how to plan a model railway, and what to base it on, if anything?

Well, for me, I always design layouts that fall into one of the three categories:

- Factually based on a real place.
- Semi-fictionally based consisting of varying amounts of fact and fiction.
- Purely, or almost purely, fictional.

I approach all three with equal enthusiasm, though it's always nice to have a break from one type when you've been focusing on it for a while.

That brings me to fictional designing, which will always have its roots set in real railway practice and locations. As such the accompanying layout design is inspired by locations in the Thames Valley: Henley-on-Thames, Windsor and Eton, Bourne End and Marlow Stations and Brunel's river bridge at Maidenhead… coupled to some scenic and track planning slight-of-hand!

The terminus at Marlow changed very little over the years, from steam to early diesel, only in 1966 was it radically remodelled with a solitary platform alongside one of the goods yard sidings. There had been a signal box to September 26 1954 and the engine shed closed July 1962, demolished 1964. ALL PICTURES (UNLESS STATED): PAUL LUNN COLLECTION.

Bourne End station as it was after the line to Wycombe had been truncated, as you can just about see from the distant buffer stop. Note the considerable size goods shed no longer in use by the railway and North Signal Box, extended in 1955, adjacent to the level crossing. Today the site is much reduced with only two platforms, though the station building and goods shed remain. There are only two points, one for the junction to Marlow, the other providing access to both platforms.

Windsor Central Station forecourt has now been converted to a shopping mall, but you can still see most of the historical architectural features as built. Opened October 8 1849, it was later completely rebuilt for Queen Victoria's Diamond Jubilee, it was used by the Royals travelling to and from Windsor Castle.

I've suggested canopies on the model track plan like that at Henley-on-Thames station, though I suspect platform length has been shortened, and a newer brick-built station building has been provided at the terminus end.

Look for detail like the running-in board here, either on-line or in books, that personalises your layout. I'm not suggesting you keep the real station names, but I certainly like the idea of adding 'JUNCTION FOR' and the wonderful fire buckets, if relevant to your chosen period.

THE PLAN

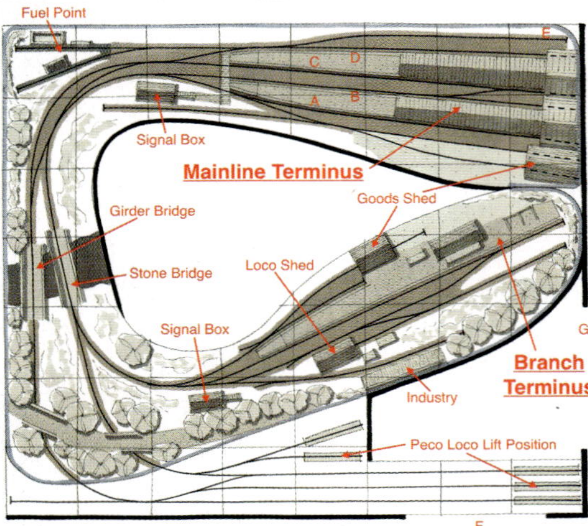

This is a compact design in a space of 8ft x 7ft for 'OO', with small central operating well, which also provides access to the fiddle yard.

The design consists of a terminus to fiddle yard arrangement with a scenic run between the two and an additional short branch line. I imagine the line to be somewhere on the outskirts of London, near the Thames, and while it almost certainly should be double track on the main line, I've opted for single lines, with a hint of double where they meet. I've done this to make the most of space and simplify point-work, both at the small terminus station and fiddle yard throat.

Additionally, I wanted to include a major scenic feature of two single track bridges, over a Thames-type river, and to explore just what might be done in terms of entry-level models. There are five roads into the terminus station, which could also be a truncated line, like Bourne End.

Be mindful of how you site the bridges (I've recommended using tried and tested Hornby models – see Step-by-Step). I wanted to be a little different rather than traditional parallel designs. I've suggested one line, built first, with the stone bridge, and the second, on a slightly deviating route. I've positioned them so the lowest and most attractive stone bridge is situated nearest the operating well and the higher girder bridge behind as a backdrop with its supporting pillars partly obscured. I must admit if I were to make the girder bridge, I'd probably dispense with the Hornby supports and build some new stone or concrete ones.

I have suggested an overall station roof, like Windsor and Eton Riverside, as a view blocker on the right-hand end.

Line A is primarily for the branch train, B C and D are main line platform faces, though D and E could be for carriage stock, at three coaches each. Note F and G are potential access doors, though with F you'd need the fiddle yard to have the last 3ft as a lift out section.

I anticipate using Code 100 Streamline and rigid geometry Setrack, the latter for curved points, top left and plain curves bottom left.

If you have slightly more space, at least an extra foot in both directions, the baseboard and track plan could be improved by the following: more gentle curves, extended track length, for greater stock capacity, and larger operating wells, for increased comfort.

Under the roof of the former London & South Western Railway's Windsor & Eaton Riverside station which provides inspiration for the main line terminus.

OPERATION

The track plan represents late steam and early diesel periods and, as such, the fuel point could either be for coal and water or diesel fuel (perhaps both). Up to a maximum of four coach trains are viable on the main line and two or three on the branch. There are wagon shunting options at both stations, though slightly more at the branch terminus, where the short bay platform can also be used for parcels, a single railcar or locomotive and autocoach.

RIGHT: The platform left served a terminating track, beyond the hedgerow, and had its own loop, closed December 11 1955, for trains to Marlow, with a Down bay starter signal on the extreme left. The arriving train was probably a special from Maidenhead on May 4 1962, hauled by an ex-GWR '14XX'. The main platform ahead is for Bourne End, or beyond to Wycombe, though reversal for Marlow was available and controlled by the down main bracket signal near the platform end. It lower signal arm was the Down Main to branch starter and the taller one is the Down Main Up starter. All was controlled from the South Signal Box to January 30 when it closed.

ABOVE: The town rises behind Windsor and Eton station and you can just make out the castle, upper left. It would make a great feature on a larger layout and where viewing could take place from outside the mainline station baseboard, but that's another story!

Nowadays with all single track, a solitary DMU covers both branch and main line duties; in the past two trains were a regular feature as here, one for the branch to Marlow and the other for the main line.

BRIDGE CONSIDERATIONS

I'm always keen to recycle and repurpose structures, particularly for those moving up or just starting at the mid, top end of entry-level, it's a great way to start or develop scratch-building skills and save money for other more expensive purchases. For this layout design I want to suggest using two of Hornby's bridges: R499 and R657, I fortunately had two of the former to hand, one a tad damaged and the other brand new. By contrast the latter is a minor adaptation by friend and modeller Peter Salmon.

For the principal arch bridge conversion I used Metcalfe M0057 stone card, and mounting card from the Range or Hobbycraft.

By using wider pillars the bridge is slightly longer and therefore a little more dramatic in its appearance, I heightened the parapet wall as the balustrade on the original looked somewhat on the low side. My main reasons for choosing this structure was the accuracy of the elliptical arch, rigidity of the structure and ethical reasons, already mentioned.

The second bridge, modelled by Peter Salmon, is a double length span. That makes it approximately the same length as my stone elliptical arch version. Peter has weathered his version, and you can see the improvement by changing the look of the original green girders with a fair amount of weathering.

Starting with the elliptical arch river bridge, as always, I look for real inspiration and one of the best examples is Brunel's Maidenhead railway bridge, opened July 1, 1839 though, unlike mine, which is single track and stone built, mainly because I might use it for a future project. That said, you can use Metcalfe brick sheet as an alternate, if that's your preference.

Hornby's old reliable arched bridge (R499)…

… And it's contemporary girder bridge (R657).

Peter Salmon's girder bridge is mainly a paint job with the addition of a fence on both sides from Hornby's elevated sidewall pack. You can clearly see the difference between the unpainted original and Peter's painted version, see more on this towards the end.

A problem with this bridge is with the incredibly out of proportion supports, which to some degree can be remedied by splitting in half and adding a central MDF packer.

1

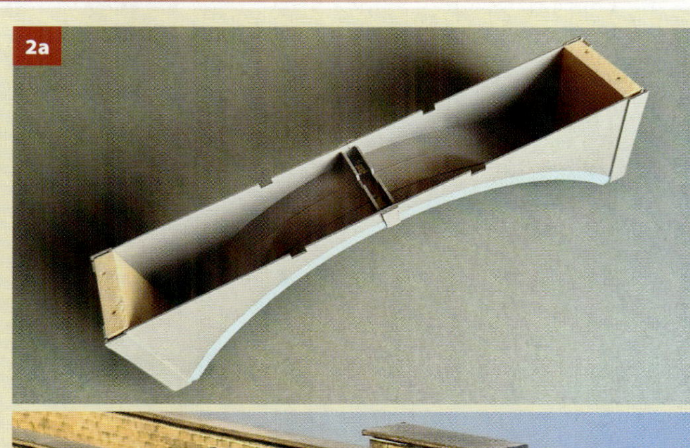

2a

2b

The elliptical stone arch bridge with its cleverly designed interlocking arch of two parts provides an ideal sub-structure and the deck with balustrades will no doubt come in use for another project, in due course.

I commenced by Super Gluing the two arch halves together and added a block of softwood to snugly fit inside both ends, which were screw-fixed through the outer ends, having countersunk the holes first. Note the hardboard deck, 322mm x 640mm is glued with PVA to the softwood uprights and screwed down into countersunk holes.

3

4

Without pillars the arch will lay flat against what is a piece of cornflakes packet, and you'll get a more accurate line. Take your pieces, you'll need one for each side, a little longer than required so they can be measured and cut, at the ends, for trimming.

Then measure the recessed arch width on the bridge and draw a second line for the full length. There's a knack to how you hold your pencil and that your second finger acts as a guide to keep the line's width accurate along its length, then cut along this new line.

5

See how the packer fits after it has been glued with PVA. Always cut away from the hand holding the card, on a cutting mat, and take your time. Practice on scrap first. Only fill the recess. Only the bottom curve needs to be really accurate. I always use a larger blade for cutting curves like these as a scalpel type can be a bit flimsy, at the pointed end.

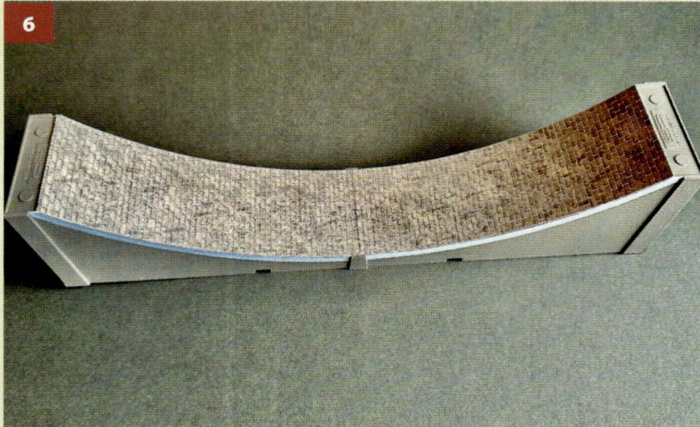

6

Cover the model in stone or brick, make sure the width is flush on both outer sides of the packers. Note the sheet joint is in the centre. With thick card, like Metcalfe's M0057 (stone), always allow for extra for wrapping round on a pillar or similar. When folding round a corner, glue the stone sheet to the largest area first and leave it to fully set before bending, otherwise the first bit will lift off. Avoid visible joins.

5

Voussoirs (main elliptical arch stones) are from thin white card and has been cut as per the packer, coloured with Windsor and Newton Promarker felt pens. I used Warm Grey 4, and using a white pencil equally divide into individual stones. Capstones are from thick white mounting card also divided into sections with a white pencil. Pencil lines will appear quite bold when first applied, but will tone down with weathering, described further on.

7a

This underside view of one end shows how I've layered mounting card for the desired thickness. The right side has two layers for the pillar, three for the packers and one for the inside. Glue the two outer pillars together and wrap stone around them with the joint at the back. Add the end capstone packer to the parapet wall, making sure the chosen height matches a number of stone course, I chose two. Note the inner, upside down, L-shaped pillar will need to be measured to fit snugly around the bridge end. Cut card squarely for better appearance and for ease of adhering to stone card. If this is too difficult, use wood, which saves on laminating: thinnest for the inner pillar, thickest for the parapet wall and medium for the outer pillars (balsa, MDF and Hardboard are all options). The diagram shows all components and principal measurements.

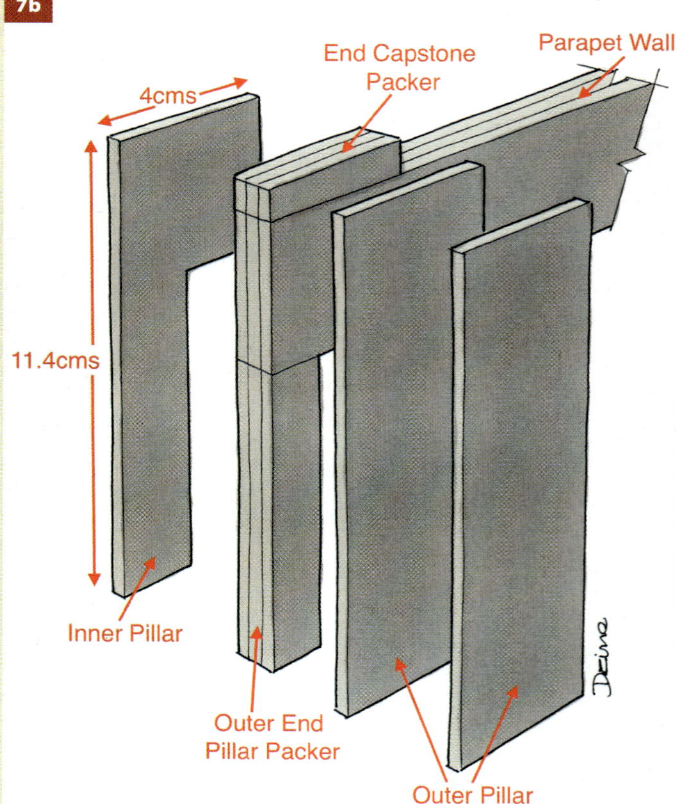

7b

9

String lines are a course or courses of stone or brick that stand out slightly from the main wall. I've put one below the capstone and one next to my lower finger. Make capstones to fit after you've added any string lines, making sure they're neither too short nor too narrow.

10

I cut staggered joints along the stone course lines when joining two pieces of Metcalfe stone sheet for the long sides (left). I made the joint at the narrowest place above the arch centre. I had difficulty maintaining accuracy and if I were to do it again, I might settle for a butt joint, which could be partially hidden by a builder's plaque. The staggered voussoirs is a test piece made before the makeover started, later discarded!

11

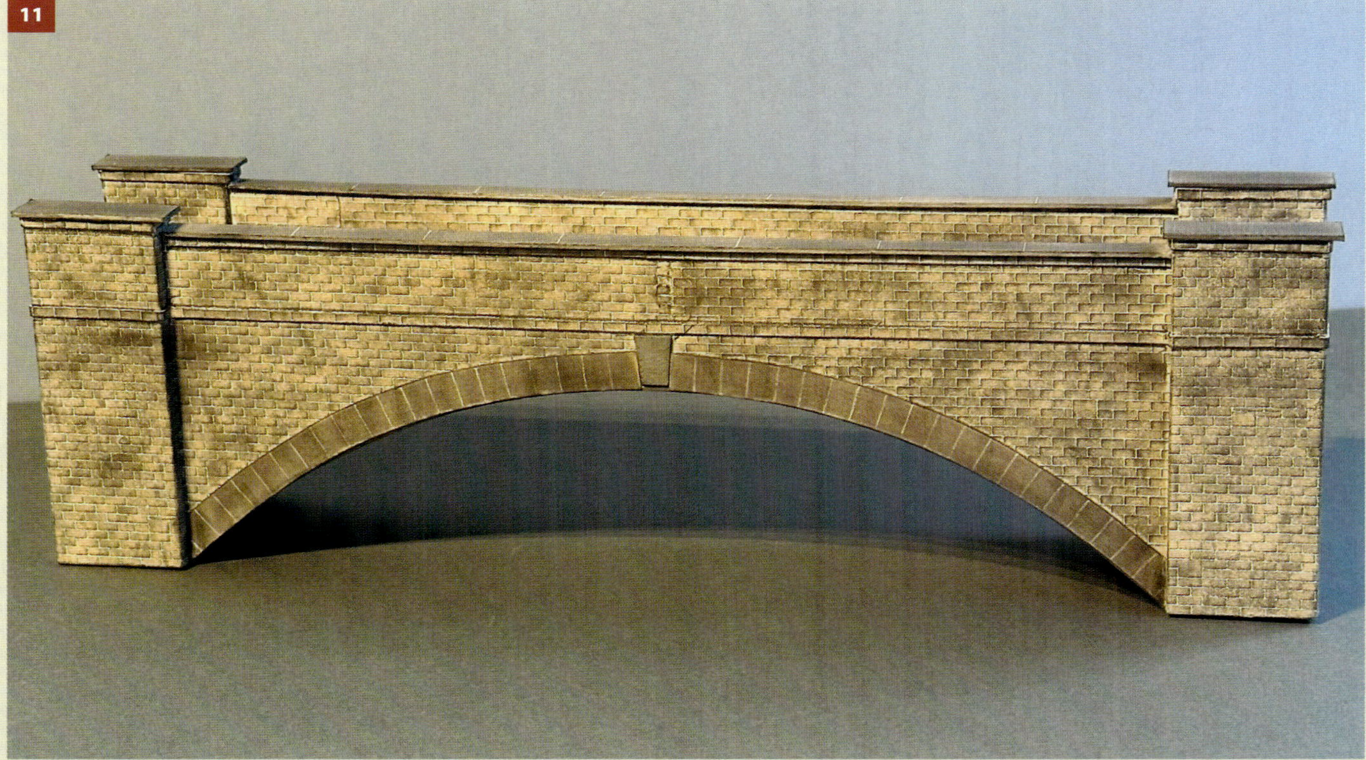

Weather stone surfaces with a cheap black artists pastel. Rub the pastel between finger and thumb and smear on to outer surface to taste. You might want to use a disposable glove to keep your fingers clean!

EXCLUSIVE PJM MODELS LASER-CUT KITS

PJM MODELS DEPOT STRUCTURES

GBRf Depot and extension kits for 'OO'

- MOD163 – Option A: **£65.99**

- MOD164 – Option B: **£55.99**

Stratford Depot four track structures for 'OO'

- MOD66 – Through depot: **£85.00**

- PJM166 – Depot and office: **£135.00**

GBRf Depot hard standing kits for 'OO'

- PJM164: **£12.99**

Derby Litchurch Lane Works modular kits for 'OO'

- **PJM165 – Base kit: £99.99**
- **PJM167 – Width extension: £49.99**
- **PJM166 – Length extension: £79.99**
- **PJM168 – Roof extension: £29.99**

PJM MODELS SIGNALBOXES

Yarnton signalbox for 'OO' gauge

- **PJM170: £32.99**

Crewe Station A for 'OO' gauge

- **PJM200: £19.99**

Exmouth Junction for 'OO' gauge

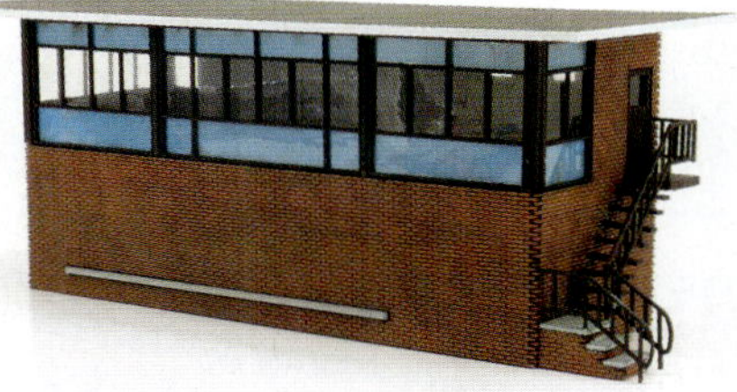

- **MOD147: £32.99**

Helpston signalbox for 'OO' gauge

- **MOD125: £32.99**

Norton Bridge signalbox for 'OO' gauge

- **MOD71: £47.99**

Norton Bridge signalbox interior for 'OO'

- **MOD78: £12.99**

WCML relay room for 'OO'

- **MOD75: £34.99**

PJM MODELS STATION SCENES

Thirsk station building for 'OO' gauge

• PJM162: **£35.99**

Single 450mm long platform with Lintel Edges for 'OO' gauge

• PJM158: **£10.99**

Triple pack of 450mm long platforms with Lintel Edges for 'OO' gauge

• PJM159: **£29.99**

Twin pack of platform ramps with Lintel Edges for 'OO' gauge

• PJM160: **£7.99**

Optional Scaffolding support pack for platforms with Lintel Edges

• PJM161: **£5.99**

Single 450mm long platform with Block Edges for 'OO' gauge

• MOD150: **£10.99**

Triple pack of 450mm long platforms with Block Edges for 'OO' gauge

• MOD151: **£29.99**

Twin pack of platform ramps with Block Edges for 'OO' gauge

• MOD152: **£7.99**

Single terminus platform section with Block Edges for 'OO' gauge

• MOD153: **£10.99**

Single 450mm long platform with Brick Edges for 'OO' gauge

• MOD154: **£10.99**

Triple pack of 450mm long platforms with Brick Edges for 'OO' gauge

• MOD155: **£29.99**

Twin pack of platform ramps with Brick Edges for 'OO' gauge

• MOD156: **£7.99**

Single terminus platform section with Brick Edges for 'OO' gauge

• PJM157: **£10.99**

Sydenham station building for 'OO' gauge

• MOD128: **£35.99**

CHECK OUT OUR FULL COLLECTION OF MODELS HERE:

keymodelworld.com/shop

977/

**3D SCANNED
3D PRINTED
MINIATURES**

BESPOKE LOCO CREWS

DETAILING COMPONENTS

...AND MUCH MORE!

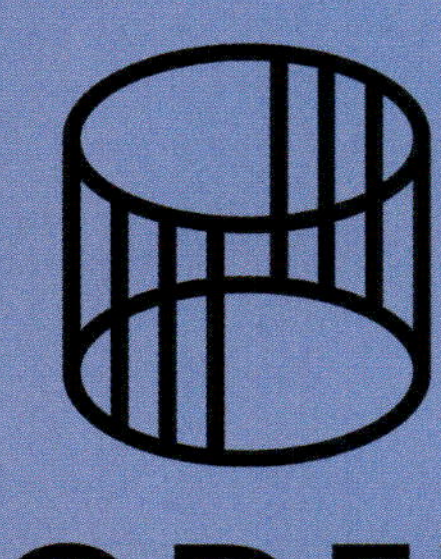

MODELU
MINIATURES

www.modelu3d.co.uk
01454 607258
Office & Workshop
40 Hounds Road
Chipping Sodbury
BS37 6EE

THE DIORAMA CHALLENGE

For Key Model World's 12th series, the Key Model World and *Hornby Magazine* team set about to craft four individual dioramas. **BEN CHURCH** outlines each of the completed scenes and details how each was designed and built.

Mike Wild combined two PJM Models kits to create a main line scene which brought together Roade Cutting and Watford Tunnel portal. A BR '9F' leads a coal train out of the gloom of the tunnel.

Railway modelling doesn't necessarily have to require vast amounts of space or even a working layout.

For the 12th Key Model World video series, the whole Key Model World and *Hornby Magazine* team decided to come together and take on a challenge to craft four unique dioramas, to not only showcase the individual modelling styles of the team, but to inspire and showcase to any modeller of any skill level, what can be achieved in a small space.

The idea came from Model World LIVE – the annual modelling event hosted by Key Publishing at the NEC in Birmingham – where model railway, scale plastic modellers and radio control modellers come together to showcase the modelling hobby. The team were wowed by the superb dioramas built by scale modellers, and particularly by how much detail could be introduced into a space as small as a tin can lid.

Our challenge had a simple brief: each of the team was given a Scalescenes 600mm x 440mm baseboard (Cat No: BB030) to work with and the ability to model whatever was desired in any scale they chose with the aim that each finished diorama showed a different vision of how the space would be used.

WATFORD TUNNEL

Mike's diorama made use of the Key Model World exclusive PJM Models 'OO' gauge Watford Tunnel portal kit (Cat No. MOD148) and Roade Cutting kit (MOD149) to craft an imposing double-track main line scene. This was then built up on the sides to create grassy hill tops, complemented by a three-quarter backscene to frame the scene.

The PJM Models Roade Cutting kit provided an excellent base for the scene, with the other elements seamlessly blended into and around it. Construction began with the kit being secured to the baseboard in the desired place. Cork was then applied to the base of the cutting to allow for a prototypical ballast shoulder to be formed. A colour light signal and cable trunking were added to enhance the lineside scene further with the cable trunking coming from the Rusty Rails Modelling range.

After ballasting the track, polystyrene was added to the top of the cutting and around the top of the tunnel, and then cut to shape to start to form contours and undulations. Plaster bandage was added on top of this to create the base for static grass and other scenic elements, such as fine leaf foliage to create dense greenery – this was also applied to the lineside, to add more colour and visual interest.

Both tracks were then weathered using an airbrush, and the substantial iron girders were then added to the top of the cutting from the PJM Models kit. A final touch was the addition of backscenes to three sides of the diorama, all painted sky blue and then drilled onto the baseboard, to frame the scene, and force an aerial or track level viewing position. Scenic choices allowed for multi-era representation, with both steam, diesel and model image models looking equally at home when posed on the two lines.

While in reality Roade Cutting and Watford Tunnel are some distance apart – in fact they are in different counties – the combination of the two West Coast Main Line inspired kits worked well together and provided a test bed for idea for future layouts.

SCRAPYARD SCENE

Jonathan Newton's diorama was born out of a heap of spare Ellis Clark Trains 'O' gauge London Midland and Scottish Railway (LMS) 'Black Five' parts, acquired from the manufacturer, with the goal of creating a scrapyard scene, reminiscent of those that so many steam locomotives met their end during BR's culling of steam.

To start, two lengths of Peco 'O' gauge track were placed on the board, followed by several layers of sand to create a texture reminiscent of the stained, undulating ground cover found in scrapyards. Foam, which was cut to shape to form a raised base for locomotive parts to be placed upon, was secured to the back of the board. The entire board was given an overall coat of black from a spray can; care

was taken to leave some of the sand's natural colour, to give a gradient to the ground cover. Humbrol weathering powders were then applied on top of the paint, to further add additional effects, the smoke, black and dark earth powders were used. These created rust effects on the surface of the board, which would then complement the rusted locomotive parts when they were secured.

The end of steam was the time setting for Jonathan Newton's scrapyard scene which sought to recreate the disposal of locomotives in the late 1960s in 'O' gauge.

Not only were a mass of Ellis Clark Trains 'Black Five' 4-6-0 parts used, but 3D printed parts from the forthcoming Clark Railworks 'OO' gauge War Department 2-10-0, which had been upscaled to 'O' gauge, plus spare parts from Ellis Clark Trains Wickham Trolley models and a selection BR Mk 1 coach parts. These were then spray-painted black and glued to the diorama in appropriate locations to build up the scene.

Some additional detail elements were added to some of the parts, with a Stanier 4000-gallon tender gaining a BR late crest, and the cabside of a 'Black Five' being given a number, both applied via waterslide transfers. Rust effects were then added to the parts in the scrapyard using Humbrol rust wash together with yellow rust and rust washes by Dirty Down. After the rust washes has dried, additional rust effects were added by using U Rust oxide grime, deep oxide and black oxide, plus more application of Humbrol weathering powders.

A final flourish was added by *Hornby Magazine* contributor Dan Evason, painting some evocative text such as 'The End' onto the 'Black Five'.

Mark Chivers' diorama took inspiration from Southern Region depots like Hither Green, but created a scene which could be stocked with a variety of motive power from different periods.

SOUTHERN DEPOT

Mark Chivers opted to craft a bustling BR era Southern Region diesel depot scene, with the PJM Models Stratford Depot through kit (Cat No. MOD66) as the centrepiece.

The first step was to shorten the depot kit, which was done using a razor saw. This gave the tracks more breathing room and allowed for additional buildings to be placed on the diorama.

DCC Concepts Legacy 'OO' gauge track was used for its more prototypical appearance offering realistic sleeper spacing and bullhead profile rail.

Track was loosely placed on the board and covered with a Scalescenes hardstanding kit, which was cut to shape to suit the shortened depot. In traditional Southern Region fashion, the depot kit was clad in corrugated metal using Wills plastic sheets to give it an entirely different appearance to how the kit was originally designed.

Additional structures were added to the diorama to fill out some empty spaces consisting of Railway Laser Lines diesel fueling point kit, plus a shunter's hut, which was constructed by Mark for a previous *Hornby Magazine* project.

Ground cover was composed almost entirely of ballast, but, before this was added, a pair of Layouts 4U yard lights were added to add height to the scene. Ballast was carefully applied around each of the buildings, giving an even, flat effect to the depot. Small tufts of grass were added at random to add additional colour.

Some BR sectorisation era doors, corrugated doors were fitted to the shed to close off some of the shed roads.

A light weathering was then applied to the track, and the scene was completed, initially with the addition of a trio of Heljan Class 33s creating an evocative Southern Region BR Sectorisation era scene. Handily the removable doors mean that the scene can be changed to different eras and provides an ideal space to display a selection of diesel locomotives from any period, as these pages prove.

STEAM SHED

Ben, also opted for a shed scene, but chose to model a small urban Great Western Railway (GWR) motive power shed, utilising a photograph of the small shed that once stood at Stratford Upon Avon in Warwickshire for inspiration.

At the centre of the scene was the Hornby Skaledale Dunster Engine Shed, providing an excellent GWR building for the scene to take place around. Three lengths of Peco Code 75 'OO' gauge track were fixed to the board, and then wired up with dropper wires, as the intention was to have Digital Command Control (DCC) sound-fitted steam locomotives simmering in the yard. A mix of woodland scenic medium and fine grey blend ballast was then added around the track.

Most of the ground cover was the Geoscenics pothole road kit, which was used to create a dirty, stained texture for a work-weary steam shed scene. This was generously applied to a majority of the scene, leaving a few small areas free of the covering. A green, unkempt area was created at one end of the scene, which featured fine leaf foliage, static grass and two large trees.

Opposite this, a Hornby Skaledale house was placed, which was enhanced with a small garden and greenhouse, the latter a Scale Model Scenery kit. PJM Models provided some prototype brick walls, which were spray-painted and secured around both the wooded area and the garden. A long wooden fence was placed alongside one side of the scene, with the addition of static grass and fine leaf foliage. A mound of coal was secured to one side of the board, which used the Geoscenics coke load kit.

Finer details were added with spare Peco sleepers, a ModelU GWR water crane and DCC Concepts gaslights, which were wired up and integrated into the DCC power for the layout. A Hornby ventilated van body was separated from the chassis and weathered with Humbrol weathering powders to create a storage unit for the shed scene. The final weathering used Humbrol weathering powders, which were mixed with water to create a black wash, which was then applied to all of the track.

An Accurascale GWR 'Manor' 4-6-0 and Bachmann '94XX' 0-6-0PT were posed on the layout to complete the scene, with the combination of the sound, firebox flicker, and working lights helping to craft the illusion of a small local shed, where locomotives can be stabled in between duties. ∎

Western Region steam in the 1960s was the setting for Ben Church's diorama which aimed to create an urban shed nestled between homes and woodland in 'OO'.

WATCH THE FULL SERIES ON KEY MODEL WORLD

Series 12 is available to watch now exclusively on Key Model World. Join the team as they build their dioramas explaining in detail how each scene was created from start to finish. Full access to this series and all of Key Model World starts from £3.99 a month giving access to more than 6,000 modelling articles, new and exclusive video series every eight weeks, back issues to 2015 and much more!

Visit *keymodelworld.com/series-12-diorama-challenge* to find out more.

150220 crosses over from the bay platform to the main line at Shortley Bridge as a Class 66 arrives behind with a cement train in the yard. **MIKE WILD**

WHAT WE USED

PRODUCT	SUPPLIER	CAT NO.
ESU LokSound V5 sound chip	roads-and-rails.co.uk	58449
Class 150 sound profile	esu.eu/en/downloads	S0400
27mm x 19mm x 13mm Midi Bass speaker	dckits-devideos.co.uk	Supersound Midi Bass
Seated passengers	Amazon	n/a
Driver	Accuracale	ACC2586

One of the inspirations for the DMU shuttle on East Coast Cement was a visit to Doncaster where Class 150/2s operated back and forth between Adwick and Sheffield. 150271 stands at Doncaster on May 22 2025. MIKE WILD

LOKSOUND HIFI CLASS 150 SOUND INSTALLATION

There is a world of choice when it comes to digital sound including a collection of HiFi sounds direct from LokSound. **MIKE WILD** explains how you can access these sound profiles and upgrades a Bachmann Class 150/2 in the process.

The ESU LokSound decoder family is exceptionally capable and has become the number one choice of digital sound chips for model railway locomotives.

But the range is more than just electronics, as the company has also been creating its own range of bespoke British outline sound files.

LokSound's own sound profiles are branded as HiFi and they are designed to offer a quality sound chip which with the project crafted in house by the ESU team. The range has expanded quickly and including classic British diesels like the Class 20, 31, 37, 47, 55, 66 and many more. They are all designed to work on the latest generation LokSound V5 decoders. The bonus is that the sound files are free which means

you can either purchase them pre-loaded onto ESU decoders from LokSound chip suppliers at a lower price or, if you have your own LokProgrammer, you can download the sounds at home and load them onto your own chips.

We wanted to test what we had heard in the audio clips available on the ESU website for the HiFi sounds by adding the project for the Class 150/2 DMU into a Bachmann two-car unit for use on the extended East Coast Cement layout. The purpose of the DMU would be to provide a shuttle running back and forth from the bay platform to the storage yard and with its collection of engine and ancillary functions the HiFi sound profile fitted the bill.

The sound was loaded onto a 21-pin ESU LokSound V5 chip via a LokProgrammer which

meant we had a 21-pin chip ready to install connected to a basic 15mm x 11mm cube speaker. Each LokSound chip comes with a cube speaker and a set of plastic components to increase the depth of its baffle, but we saw there was room to install a bigger speaker with a small compromise to the interior space.

To take the project a few steps further we also added a collection of passengers to the interior, a driver and light weathering to model a recently repainted Northern Rail unit with smart bodysides combined with a toned down underframe and roof.

The following step by step guide explains how we did it and you can watch a video demonstration of the finished model at *keymodelworld.com/digital-sound* ∎

STEP BY STEP | **INSTALLING ESU HIFI SOUND IN THE BACHMANN CLASS 150/2**

The Bachmann Class 150/2 is smartly presented in Northern Rail livery as 150220 for 'OO' gauge and will be even better with the addition of sound, passengers, a driver and light weathering.

To separate the bodies from the chassis there are three screws in the chassis that need to be released – all three are crosshead screws. The first two are at the rear either side of the coupling mount.

The third body fixing screw is located underneath the leading bogie of each coach. Turn the bogie to one side to access the screw.

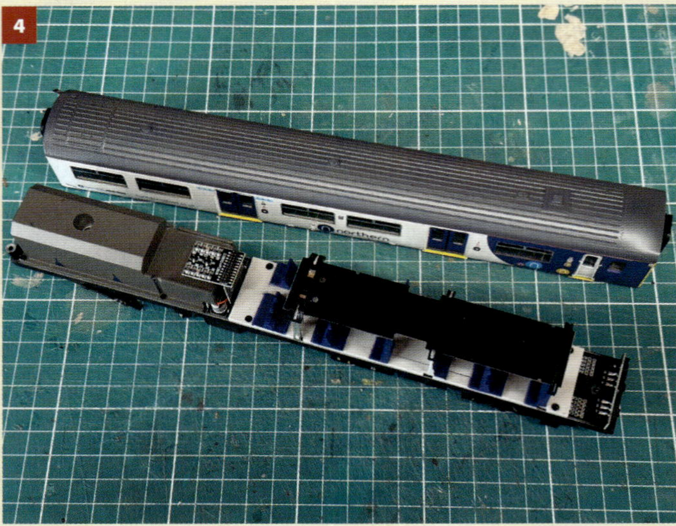

With the body offer the interior layout is clear to see. There is limited space inside for a hidden speaker, but there is a handy 21-pin socket which powers the motor and lighting functions.

This DCC ready model needs the 21-pin blanking plug removing from the socket which is located on top of a vertically positioned Printed Circuit Board (PCB).

The ESU LokSound V5 21-pin chip comes with a 15mm x 11mm cube speaker pre-wired to the decoder. Our chip has already been loaded with the ESU HiFi sound for the Class 150/2 DMU.

Fitting the decoder takes seconds as it plugs firmly onto the 21-pin socket in the DMU. However, we saw space to add a larger more powerful speaker to improve its sound output.

To enhance the sound output we chose a 27mm x 19mm x 13mm Midi Bass speaker from DC Kits to install in the DMU in place of the original 15mm x 11mm cube.

The location for the speaker will be across the rear most seats in the motorised car – a compromise in terms of appearance, but one which will provide a quality sound output.

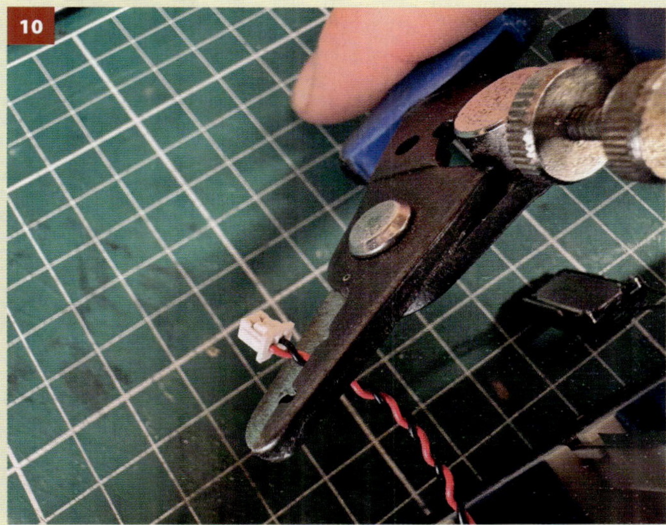

To connect the speaker we are going to attach the red and black wires to the brown wires from the decoder to avoid soldering on the chip. The first step is to remove the plug

Similarly the brown wires to the original speaker with the chip need to be cut so that we can use them to power the new speaker.

To ensure the join between the wires is fully insulated we slotted two 15mm lengths of heatshrink insulation over the brown wires prior to twisting the speaker wires together.

Nexct the red and black wires from the speaker were twisted onto the brown wires from the decoder to complete the circuit.

To make this joint permanent, the twisted wires were soldered together to create a strong and consistent bond between them.

Now the important part – the heatshrink insulation was moved up and over the soldered joint and then reduced in size using the side of a soldering iron.

The completed connections are now fully insulated protecting the wires from short circuits which ensures there can be no damage to the DCC decoder.

The speaker was then positioned as planned at the rear of the passenger compartment. It is held in place with Black Tack for a strong fixing.

To make a little more of the Class 150 we wanted to add a driver and passengers. To fit a driver the cab interior needs unclipped from the body.

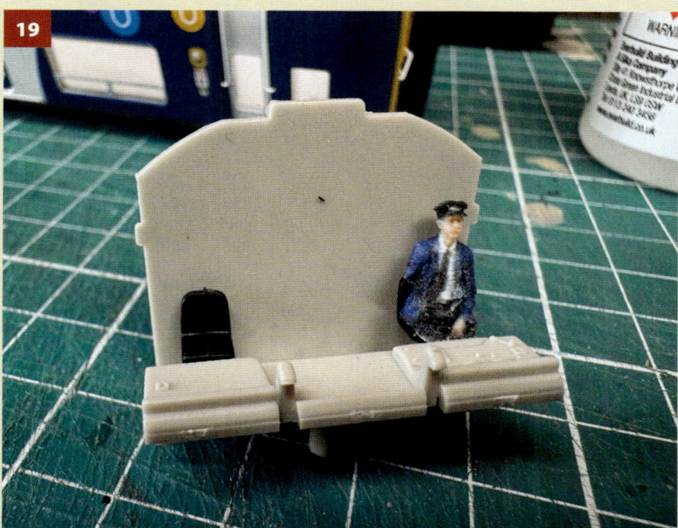

We used a pre-coloured 3D-printed driver from Accurascale in the Class 150 which sat neatly on the driver's seat in the cab.

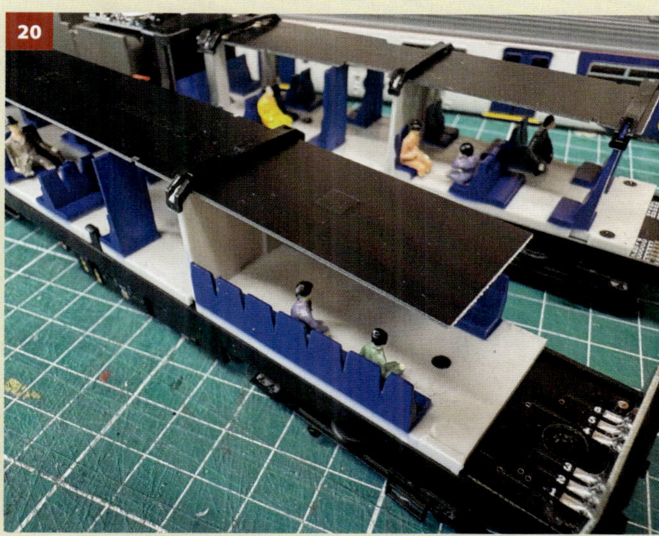

Similarly, passengers were added to the unit using a set of pre-painted seated figures. In all cases the legs of these passengers needed shortening to fit the seating unit in the Class 150.

The Class 150 comes with optional miniature snowploughs and a choice of working or static BSI couplings. We fitted the ploughs and static couplings at each end to complete its exterior.

Next the unit moved across into the paint booth for a light weathering – nothing over the top, but enough to tone down the factory fresh finish to represent a well maintained in service unit. The first colour is Lifecolor LPW24 Frame Dirt from the Liquid Pigments Trains and Tracks set (LP05).

The roof was then toned down with Carriage Grime (LPW22) from the same set of Lifecolour paints. A number of passes were made along the length of the coach roof adding tone and texture.

The finishing touch was to add dirt spatter on the cab front which represents the dirt that the units would pick up in service. At this stage the paints are still drying, but once complete 150220 will look the part for East Coast Cement.

QUITE ALL WIGHT!

From Victorian branch lines to second hand Underground stock, the Isle of Wight's unique railway history has long captured modellers' imaginations – and manufacturers have responded with an unprecedented range of ready-to-run offerings. **NICK BRODRICK** reports.

MAIN: Modelling a typical Isle of Wight passenger train of the 1940s will soon be possible thanks to EFE Rail's forthcoming Brighton-built bogie carriages (of the type shown in the lead two vehicles) to match its extant 'O2' tanks. The trailing Chatham bogie brake is not yet available in ready-to-run form, but Rapido's Evolution stock might provide a neat solution. On November 20 2023, the Isle of Wight Steam Railway's flagship engine W24 *Calbourne* approaches Havenstreet with a train from Smallbrook Junction. **NICK BRODRICK**.

RIGHT: *Calbourne*'s forever home is Havenstreet, but you can take one of its miniature versions home from the Isle of Wight Steam Railway gift shop! **IWSR**.

The diamond-shaped Isle of Wight, measuring just 23 miles by 13, once boasted an extraordinary 55.5 miles of line. Today, only 8.5 miles of operational track remains (between Ryde and Shanklin) as part of the national network.

The island's railway heritage lives on through preservation efforts and, increasingly, through the dedication of model manufacturers who've recognised the unique appeal of this maritime railway system.

The island's railway story began on June 16 1862 when the Cowes & Newport Railway opened its 4.5-mile line after nearly three years of construction. This modest beginning sparked a boom that would see the island criss-crossed with lines by the turn of the century. The Isle of Wight Railway (IWR) followed in 1864 with its line from Ryde to Sandown, extended to Ventnor in 1866, creating the spine of what would become the island's most enduring 'main line' route.

By 1901, the network had reached its zenith. Multiple companies – the IWR, Isle of Wight Central Railway (IWCR), and Freshwater, Yarmouth & Newport Railway (FYNR) – operated services that connected every significant town and village.

Tourists flocked to Victorian resorts via rail, while local traffic sustained a surprisingly intensive service pattern. The peculiar sight of ex-London suburban and carriages operating on what were essentially secondary and rural branch lines gave the island's railways much of their distinctive character, especially as mainland railways modernised.

The 1923 Grouping had brought the disparate operations under Southern Railway control, initiating a programme of standardisation and modernisation, coinciding with the beginning of a golden inter-war era fuelled by ever-increasing

Top dogs! 'Terrier' No. W11 (named *Newport* part way through its SR life) runs through Ashey Halt on November 21 2023. **NICK BRODRICK**.

holiday demand. Comparatively ancient locomotives gave way to more modern types, primarily the ex-London South Western Railway Adams 'O2' 0-4-4Ts, while a fleet of bogie coaches built by the London, Brighton & South Coast Railway found new life on the island.

UNDERGROUND… OVERGROUND

Decline came swiftly after nationalisation. Between 1952 and 1966, line after line succumbed to closure, until only the 8.5-mile section from Ryde Pier Head to Shanklin survived (the section to Ventnor closing in April 1966).

The final day of steam operation, December 31 1966, coincided with the end of the Victorian 'O2' tanks, which had become the last pre-Grouping locomotives to haul BR passenger trains anywhere.

What followed was a unique form modernisation, very much in keeping with the island's tradition for re-homing 'Londoners'.

The physical constraints of Ryde Tunnel, whose floor had been raised to prevent flooding, meant conventional DMUs couldn't be used without major (and impractical) modifications. British Rail's solution was inspired if unconventional – second-hand London Underground deep-tube stock.

Third rail was laid and platforms lowered to accommodate 1923-built 'Standard' stock (classified as Classes 485/486) which crossed over the Solent to begin the modernised(!) passenger services in spring 1967.

After rejecting 1938 stock in 1973 owing to maintenance concerns, the railway struggled

ABOVE: The Isle of Wight Central Railway might be long gone, but its colourful memory has been brought back to life with Hornby's delightful little 'A1X' 11 and a train of (generic) varnished teak four-wheelers…
BELOW: … As well as the earlier, red liveried 'A1' 10 (later SR W10 *Cowes*). Both: **HORNBY**.

It's remarkable to think that virtually all the trains – and building – in this Havenstreet scene will soon be available in 'OO' – 'Terrier', 'O2', LBSCR bogie coaches and the station building. Even the ex-London, Chatham and Dover Railway four-wheel carriage (left) can be represented using the former Hattons Genesis coach range. Visting 0-6-0T W14 *Bembridge* meets resident 0-4-4T W24 *Calbourne* in June 2021. **NICK BRODRICK**.

RIGHT: Even though London Underground trains have been a fixture of Isle of Wight Railways for nearly 60 years, they still cut an unusual shape. After retirement from SouthWest Trains' Island Line service, unit 483007 *Jess Harper* was presented to the Isle of Wight Steam Railway for preservation and is displayed in Train Story. NICK BRODRICK.

Tooling for a game-changing selection of LBSCR-built 54ft bogie carriages – essential for any 1930s-1960s layout – has already been completed by Bachmann's EFE brand. EFE.

on with the increasingly decrepit units until 1989; their condition not helped by the corrosive effects of running just above sea water on Ryde Pier. In a further remarkable transformation, extensively refurbished 1938 stock arrived from Eastleigh Works. These trains, designated Class 483, would serve the island for over three decades until their retirement in January 2021, when they held the distinction of being Britain's oldest passenger trains in regular service.

Their replacement was a third generation of reconditioned Undergound Stock; five D78 two car units which have been converted by Vivarail into the 'D Train' Class 484s.

PRESERVATION PIONEERS

Steam hasn't been forgotten for the last six decades though. Far from it.

Indeed, even before the last of its type departed from passenger service in 1966, preservation efforts were underway. The Wight Locomotive Society, formed in 1967, secured 'O2' 0-4-4T W24 *Calbourne*, which was fortuitously retained by BR for engineering duties in the lead up to electrification. This 1891-built locomotive, the last surviving example of its class, became the cornerstone of preservation efforts, together with a rake of LBSCR and South Eastern Chatham Railway carriages.

In 1971, the society established itself at Havenstreet station (on the former Ryde – Cowes route), eventually evolving as the Isle of Wight Steam Railway (IWSR). That year, *Calbourne* hauled historic carriages from Newport to their new home and subsequently pulled the first passenger trains

"Tourists flocked to Victorian resorts via rail, while local traffic sustained a surprisingly intensive service pattern"

Havenstreet station is now available as a limited edition from the Bachmann Scenecraft collection. **BACHMANN**.

on the preserved line. Today, the railway operates 5.5 miles through quintessential Wight countryside, meticulously recreating a Southern Railway atmosphere.

The preserved line's locomotive roster has expanded to include repatriated Stroudley 'Terriers' W8 *Freshwater* and W11 *Newport*, as well as a non-native Hawthorn Leslie 0-4-0ST, Hunslet Austerity 0-6-0STs and LMS-design Ivatt 2-6-2Ts.

However, a future homogenous addition will be LBSCR 'E1' W2 *Yarmouth*; replicating the long scrapped original using classmate (and sole remaining 'E1') 110 *Burgundy* as the basis.

The line can also call on ex-BR Island Line Class 03 and 05 diesel shunters, plus the quirk of the restored Ryde Pier Drewery tram.

The range of rolling stock has expanded too.

Dozens of old four and six-wheel carriage bodies found second uses, dotted around the Isle of Wight after withdrawal. Eight – and counting – of these hen houses and holiday chalets have been beautifully restored to passenger carrying use, using second-hand SR parcels van underframes in most cases.

Kernow Model Centre filled an important gap in 2022 with LSWR 10 Ton goods brake van. It has since added LBSCR five-plank opens to its island offerings. **HM**.

MODELLING RENAISSANCE

The unique character of Isle of Wight railways has long attracted modellers, although the most successful layouts have required considerable skill and patience to fill the many rolling stock gaps.

However, in recent years, the 'OO' audience has witnessed an unprecedented expansion in ready-to-run offerings. Where once enthusiasts relied on kit-building skills or expensive commissions, today's modeller can choose from an impressive array of authentic locomotives, coaches, and wagons.

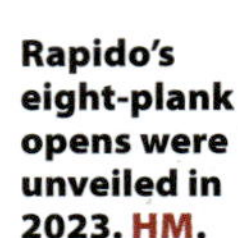

Rapido's eight-plank opens were unveiled in 2023. **HM**.

The Isle of Wight models are coming thick and fast! Bulleid-style malachite green 0-6-0T No. 1 *Medina* is one of Rapido's acclaimed 'E1' new-tooling releases in 2025. **RAPDIO**.

The island's reputation as a retirement home continues to be upheld, even by locomotives. Joining historic 'Terrier' 11 are 'Austerity' 198 Royal Engineer and Ivatt 41313. **NICK BRODRICK**.

Hornby leads the historical timeline with its lined-red IWCR 'A1' W10, representing the 'Terriers' that were prevalent in the first half of the 20th Century.

An 'A1X' plus three coach pack includes lined-black 'A1X' 11 with matching varnished teak stock using Hornby's generic four-wheelers.

Other Isle of Wight style four-wheelers in SR olive green have been offered from both the Margate manufacturer and the sadly defunct Hattons. Matching these have been a clutch of 'Terriers' – W9 *Fishbourne* (Rails of Sheffield), W10 *Cowes* and W14 *Bembridge* (both Hornby).

For post-war SR modellers, Hornby's W13 *Carisbrooke* shows off the vibrant Bulleid malachite green with British Railways patched lettering.

'O2' BE BACK AGAIN!

Bachmann's EFE Rail brand has also helped the Isle of Wight modelling revolution.

Using former DJ Models tooling, a variety of island 'O2s' have been offered, in SR olive and malachite, and BR lined black. Like the former Ryde and Newport allocated tank engines, these models differ from their mainland counterparts with Westinghouse air brake pumps and tanks, and extended bunkers.

EFE's March 2025 announcement of comprehensive LBSCR bogie-coach packs addressed a long-standing gap in the market. These four-coach sets replicate the 60 coaches transferred to the island between 1936 and 1939, featuring the most common diagrams: six-compartment Brake Thirds, seven-compartment Brake Thirds, nine-compartment Thirds, and eight-compartment Composites.

The last two decades of steam operation relied on these and ex-SECR stock running in mixed rakes of up to six vehicles. While it seems inevitable that such models will be also offered, those less patient might look to Rapido's promised Evolution range of generic pre-Grouping bogie carriages with lined olive and malachite versions planned for its elliptical-roof pattern examples – a reasonable match for the Ashford design.

EFE is also responsible for a selection of 1938 'Tube Trains' ideal for Island Line's late 1980s-2020 era, but only London-specific prototypes have been hitherto available as part of the motorised range.

In 2025, Rapido Trains launched its much-anticipated 'E1' models, with Island examples turned out in SR olive, wartime black, post-war BR malachite green and unlined BR black.

WIGHT GOODS

Kernow Model Rail Centre contributes ex-LBSCR five-plank wagons; essential for post-Grouping era modellers with 450 full size examples shipped to the island between 1924 and 1947.

The Cornish model store has already offered similarly ubiquitous LSWR 'Road Vans' (single end veranda brake vans).

Rapido has also addressed Wight goods traffic with its recent announcement of ex-LBSCR 8-ton covered vans. These Diagram D8 vehicles saw nearly 50 examples transferred to the island. Many survived until the end of steam, with three now preserved.

That good news follows the same company's earlier offering of SR eight-plank open wagons, 88 of which were shipped across the Solent.

It isn't only rolling stock that has received attention from the major manufacturers' shrink-rays. Havenstreet's Grade II-Listed all in one station and signalbox is available thanks to Bachmann Scenecraft whose delightful resin model is offered as an Isle of Wight Steam Railway exclusive.

So far, this is the only 'ready-to-plonk' building for 'OO', meaning scratch building is the way to go if you want to recreate any of the island's other classic locations, whether that's Freshwater, Cowes, Ventnor or Ryde.

Wherever takes your fancy, the current golden age of RTR means this unique system can now be recreated with unprecedented accuracy with the tools now here to bring the island to life in miniature. For those seeking something different from mainstream modelling subjects, the Isle of Wight offers charm, character, and now, comprehensive commercial support. ■

WHAT IS AVAILABLE IN OTHER GAUGES?

'N' gauge modellers have a few options from the RTR world to kick start an island layout.

Dapol's tiny 'Terrier' tooling caters for the engines that gained extended bunkers (such as W8 *Freshwater*); while Revolution Trains is promising the two-car Class 483 in both Network SouthEast colours and final Island Line red. Complementing the late 19802/early 1900s era is Kernow Model Centre's limited edition Graham Farish Class 03 disel shunter 03179.

Remarkably, the newest British scale – 'TT:120' – will soon boast its own Isle of Wight train. The 2025 range of 'Terriers' includes W14 *Bembridge* and four different types of LBSCR four-wheelers in, all in SR olive green.

Exactly the same combination already exists for 'O' gauge fans – the offered 'Terrier' is W9 *Fishbourne*.

DC Rail Freight
56091

YOUR MODELLING DESTINATION

THE UNITED
STEEL
COMPANIES LTD
SCUNTHORPE
18
18

Forward to 2026

From 'N' to 'TT:120', 'OO' to 'O', it's been another busting year of product announcements. **NICK BRODRICK** gets the lowdown of what locomotives, units, carriages and wagons we can look forward to in 2026 and beyond.

Accurascale has already shown off decorated samples of its 'OO' gauge 'Austerity' saddle tanks, including NCB North West *Warrior* and Gisel exhaust fitted *United Steel Company 18*. **MIKE WILD**

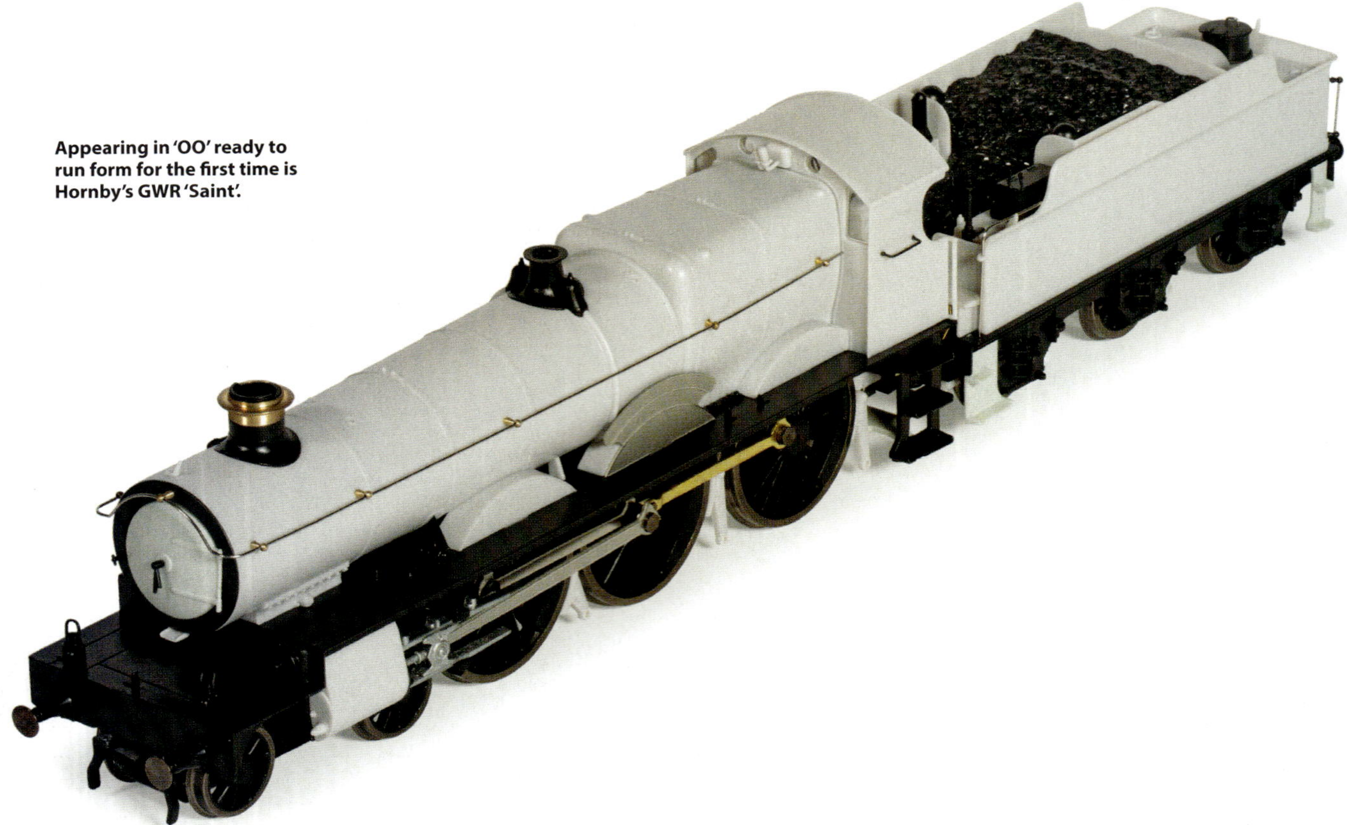

Appearing in 'OO' ready to run form for the first time is Hornby's GWR 'Saint'.

There are 52 weeks in a year… and there are just about as many new model announcements. Picking up *Hornby Magazine* each month attests to this fact. A glut of four, five, sometimes six, all new ready-to-run rolling stock toolings are unveiled each issue. It can be difficult to keep track – and so this one-stop guide will help plan your next investments.

The breadth of available models – from 1825 to contemporary multiple units – ensures every modelling interest finds representation.

As we move into a new year, the foundations laid in 2025 releases suggest sustained innovation and growth. New entrants continue raising quality expectations while established manufacturers respond with ambitious programmes. The success of specialised subjects and limited runs demonstrates market maturity supporting diversity rather than demanding mass production as was once prevalent.

The collaboration between manufacturers, retailers, preservation groups, and the modelling community has created a golden age of choice and quality. Technical innovation, manufacturing excellence, and market understanding combine to serve an engaged community of modellers.

With that thought in mind, let's crack on with the lowdown of what new ready-to-run products are expected in 2026 onwards.

'OO' GAUGE

Hornby's 2025 range announcements headlined with a newly tooled GWR 'Saint' 4-6-0. Initial releases include preservation replica 2999 *Lady*

Heljan's LNER Garratt is shaping up to be one of the most impressive steam outline models ever offered in 'OO'.

Dapol's high-spec 'OO' Southern 'Light Pacifics' bristle with detail and features.

of *Legend* and 2975 *Lord Palmer*, both in lined Great Western green with square-section frames.

The GWR's first 4-6-0 will be joined by its last – the Hawksworth 'County' – thanks to Rapido.

Pre-Grouping subjects dominated the 2024/5 announcements. Most notably, it was Scottish modellers who had the most to be excited by. Rapido Trains UK's Highland Railway 'Loch' 4-4-0 will follow on from its popular 'Jones Goods' 4-6-0, while its Great North of Scotland Railway 'V'/'F' (LNER 'D40') adds a new company to RTR ranges for the first time. These elegant 4-4-0 are also being offered as a South Eastern & Chatham Railway/Southern Railway 'G' class exclusive through Rails of Sheffield (RoS).

The Scottish bonanza continued with Rapdio's left field reveal of the one-off Caledonian

'00' GAUE NEW MOTIVE POWER PROJECTS 2025 FORWARDS			
PRODUCT	**REGION**	**MANUFACTURER**	**EXPECTED**
Ivor the Engine	Wales	Rapido Trains UK	TBA
GWR '28XX' 2-8-0	Western	Dapol	TBA
GWR '2884' 2-8-0	Western	Dapol	TBA
GWR '57XX' 0-6-0PT	Western	Accurascale	TBA
GWR '67XX' 0-6-0PT	Western	Accurascale	TBA
GWR '8750' 0-6-0PT	Western	Accurascale	2025
GWR '58XX'/'14XX'	Western	Dapol	2026
GWR 'Saint' 4-6-0	Western	Hornby	2025
GWR 'County' 4-6-0	Western	Rapido Trains UK	TBA
LBSCR 'K' 2-6-0	Southern	Sonic Models	2026
LSWR 'T3' 4-4-0	Southern	EFE Rail	2025
LSWR 'B4' 0-4-0T	Southern	Hornby Railroad	TBA
SECR 'G' 4-4-0	Southern	Rapido Trains UK	TBA
SR 'U' 2-6-0	Southern	Rapido Trains UK	TBA
SR 'WC'/'BB' 4-6-2	Southern	Dapol	2026
MR '483' 4-4-0	Midland	Rapido Trian UK	TBA
MR 'Big Bertha' 0-10-0	Midland	KR Models	TBA
GNSR 'V'/'F' ('D40')	Scottish	Rapido Trains UK	TBA
CR 'Single'	Scottish	Rapido Trains UK	TBA
HR 'Loch' 4-4-0	Scottish	Rapido Trains UK	TBA
LYR 'Pug' 0-4-0ST	Midland	Clark Railworks	2026/7
LMS '8F' 2-8-0	Midland	Bachmann	2026
NBR 'K' ('D34') 4-4-0	Scottish	Sonic	2026
GNR 'J13' ('J52/2') 0-6-0ST	Eastern	Rapido Trains UK	TBA
NER 'E' ('J71') 0-6-0T	Eastern	Bachmann	2026
LNER 'U1' 2-8-0+0-8-2	Eastern	Heljan	2025
USATC 'S160' 2-8-0	Various	Rapido Trains UK	2025
WD 'Austerity' 0-6-0ST	Various/industrial	Accurascale	TBA
WD 'Austerity' 2-10-0	Various	Ellis Clark Trains	TBA
WD 'Austerity' 2-10-0	Various	KR Models	TBA
Port of Par Bagnall 0-4-0ST	Industrial	Rapido Trains UK	2025
Haydock Foundry 0-6-0WT	Industrial	KR Models	2025
Manning Wardle 'L' 0-6-0ST	Industrial	Rapido Trains UK	TBA
Andrew Barclay Fireless 0-4-0	Industrial	Rapido Trains UK	2025
GSR '800' 4-6-0	Ireland	Irish Railway Models	2026
Prototype 'Deltic' Co-Co	Eastern/Midland	Hornby	2025
Class 04 Drewry 0-6-0 diesel shunter	Eastern/Southern	Rapido Trains UK	Postponed
Class 18 Clayton CBD90 Bo-Bo	Industrial	Revolution Trains	TBA
Class 40 1Co-Co1	Midland/Eastern	KR Models	TBA
Class 47 Co-Co	Various	Cavelex	TBA
Class 42 'Warship' Bo-Bo	Western	Heljan	2025
Class 44 1-Co-Co-1	Midland	Heljan	TBA
Class 66 Co-Co	Various	Bachmann	2025
Class 74 Bo-Bo electric	Southern	EFE Rail	TBA
Class 86/2 Bo-Bo electric	Midland/Eastern	Heljan	2026
Class 93 tri-mode Bo-Bo	Rail Ops Group	Revolution Trains	TBA
Class 99 bi-mode Co-Co	GBRf	Revolution Trains	TBA
Class 142 two-car DMU	Midland/Eastern	Realtrack	2025
Clas 153 single-car DMU	Various	Heljan	TBA
Class 155 two-car DMU	Eastern	Heljan	2025
Class 175 two-car DMU	Midland/Wales	Revolution Trains	TBA
Class 175 three-car DMU	Midland/Wales	Revolution Trains	TBA
Class 180 five-car DMU	Various	Revolution Trains	2025
Class 320 three-car EMU	Scottish	Revolution Trains	2026
Class 321 four-car EMU	Midland/Eastern	Revolution Trains	2026
Class 323 three-car EMU	Midland	Dapol	2025
Class 375/377/379/387 'Electrostar' EMU	Various	Accurscale	TBA
Class 800 IET	Various	Hornby Railroad	TBA
4-DD four-car EMU	Southern	KR Models	2025
Hunslet 0-6-0DH	Industrial	Revolution Trains	2026
IE Class 22000 Railcars	IE/Ireland	Irish Railway Models	TBA
TOTAL: 61 STEAM: 35 DIESEL/ELECTRIC: 26			

The EFE Class 74 is not far from production for 'OO' collectors.

'Single' 4-2-2 No. 123, while Sonic Models and RoS are teaming-up to bring the North British Railway 'K' ('D34') 4-4-0 to market.

London Midland Region fans also have a tiny Lancashire & Yorkshire Railway 0-4-0ST 'Pug' to look forward to courtesy of Clark Railworks.

Bachmann Branchline's new Stanier '8F' 2-8-0 fills a significant gap: the LMS workhorse saw wartime deployment across most regions, and into the Middle East and North Africa, with tooling accommodating both wartime austerity and peacetime configurations.

Bachmann is doing its bit too with an all-new North Eastern 'E' ('J71') 0-6-0T, designed by Thomas William Worsdell, to complement its related Wilson Worsdell 'E1' ('J72').

Hornby followed Rapido's 'J13' ('J52/2') announcement with subtly different, earlier 'J52' variant. Despite being

Little 'Pug' and big 'Pug'! Clark Railworks Lancashire & Yorkshire 0-4-0STs are at the tooling and 3D-printed sample stages in 'O' and 'OO' respectively.

Heljan's engineering prototype sample for its forthcoming 'OO' gauge Class 153 DMU.

Clark Railworks' much-anticipated 'Dub Dee' 2-10-0s in 'OO' will come in a host of guises, including this *Hornby Magazine* exclusive Longmoor Military Railway blue 60 Gordon.

'OO' GAUGE NEW ROLLING STOCK PROJECTS 2025 FORWARDS

PRODUCT	REGION	MANUFACTURER	EXPECTED
'Evolution' 48ft carriages	Any	Rapido Trains UK	2025
GWR Diagram N Autocoach	Western	Dapol	2025
CIE Park Royal D176 carriages	CIE/IR Ireland	Irish Railway Models	TBA
LBSCR 54ft four-coach Isle of Wight pack (Brake Thirds, Third and Composite)	Southern	EFE Rail	2025
Bulleid 'Tavern Car' Dia 2663	Southern	Hornby	2026
Bulleid 'Tavern Car' Dia 2665	Southern	Hornby	2026
Bulleid Dia 2406 Brake Corridor Third	Southern	Bachmann	2026
Bulleid Dia 2017 Third Open	Southern	Bachmann	2026
BR(E) 'BZ' six-wheel van	Eastern	The Model Centre	TBA
GWR 'Macaw B' bogie bolster	Western	Hornby	Postponed
GWR 'O19' 'Tube' wagon	Western	Rapido Trains UK	TBA
GWR 'Totem A' wagon	Western	Oxford Rail	TBA
LBSCR 8ton van	Southern	Rapdio	TBA
LNWR four-plank open wagon	Midland	Rapido	TBA
LMS 20ton brake van	Midland	Bachmann	2025
LMS box van	Midland	Rapido Trains UK	TBA
LMS 20ton hopper wagon	Midland	Rapido Trains UK	TBA
GER five-plank open wagon	Eastern	Rapido Trains UK	TBA
GNR 8ton box van	Eastern	Rapido Trains UK	TBA
NER/LNER 20ton coal hopper	Eastern	Accurascale	TBA
RCH 1907 salt wagons Rapido	Various	Rapido Trains UK	TBA
BR china clay open 'Hood'	Western/Midland	Accurascale	2025
BR 'Prestwin' wagon	Various	Clark Railworks	2025
BR 'Borail B' bogie wagon	Various	Revolution Trains	TBA
BR 'Borail C' bogie wagon	Various	Revolution Trains	TBA
BR 'YQA' 'Parr' bogie wagon	Various	Revolution Trains	2025
BR 'YQA' 'Super Tench' wagon	Various	Revolution Trains	2025
BIA/BWA/BXA/BZA covered steel carrier	Various	Revolution Trains	2025
Ministry of Munitions chemical tank	Various	Rapido Trains UK	TBA
Cowans Sheldon 15ton crane	Various	Oxford Rail	TBA
FCA/FYA 60ft intermodal wagon	Various	Accurascale	2025
PXA steel coil wagon	Various	Cavelex	2025
JXA steel scrap wagon	Various	Cavelex	2025

TOTAL: 33

'O' GAUGE NEW MOTIVE POWER PROJECTS 2025 FORWARDS

PRODUCT	REGION	MANUFACTURER	EXPECTED
SR 'USA' 0-6-0T	Southern	Minerva Models	TBA
LYR 'Pug' 0-4-0ST	Midland	Clark Railworks	2026
LMS '2MT' 2-6-2T	Midland	Lionheart Trains	2026
LNER 'J70' 0-6-0T	Eastern	Rapido Trains UK	TBA
Class 66 Co-Co	Various	Dapol	2026
Class 121 single-car DMU	Western/Midland	Heljan	TBA
Class 122 single-car DMU	Western/Midland	Heljan	TBA
Class 149 trailer car	Western/Midland	Heljan	TBA
Class 150 trailer car	Western/Midland	Heljan	TBA

TOTAL: 9 STEAM: 4 DIESEL/ELECTRIC: 5

'O' GAUGE ROLLING STOCK PROJECTS 2025 FORWARDS

PRODUCT	REGION	MANUFACTURER	EXPECTED
GWR 'M'/'M4' shunter's truck	Western	Dapol	2025
ZUA 'Shark' ballast plough	Various	Clark Railworks	Postponed

TOTAL: 2

'N' GAUGE MOTIVE POWER PROJECTS 2025 FORWARDS

PRODUCT	REGION	MANUFACTURER	EXPECTED
GWR '7800' 'Manor' 4-6-0	Western	Dapol	2025
GWR 'Hall' 4-6-0	Western	Graham Farish	2026
GWR 'Modified Hall' 4-6-0	Western	Graham Farish	2026
SR air-smoothed 'WC'/'BB' 4-6-2	Southern	Dapol	2026
SR rebuilt 'WC'/'BB' 4-6-2	Southern	Dapol	2026
LMS '2MT' 2-6-2T (upgrade)	Midland	Dapol	2025
GCR 'A5' 4-6-4T	Eastern	Sonic Models	2026
LNER 'J72' 0-6-0T	Eastern	Dapol	2026
LNER 'V2' 2-6-2	Eastern	Graham Farish	2026
Class 56 Co-Co (retool)	Various	Dapol	TBA
Class 66 Co-Co	Various	Dapol	TBA
Class 69 Co-Co	Various	Graham Farish	TBA
Class 87 Bo-Bo electric	Midland	Dapol	TBA
Class 120 Swindon cross-county DMU	Western	Revolution Trains	TBA
Class 175 two-car DMU	Midlands/Wales	Revolution Trains	TBA
Class 175 three-car DMU	Midlands/Wales	Revolution Trains	2025
Class 180 five-car DMU	Various	Revolution Trains	2025
Class 313/314 EMU	Various	Revolution Trains	2025
Class 377 Electrostar EMU	Western/Southern	Revolution Trains	2026
LT 1938 tube stock	London	Revolution Trains	2025

TOTAL: 20 STEAM: 9 DIESEL/ELECTRIC: 11

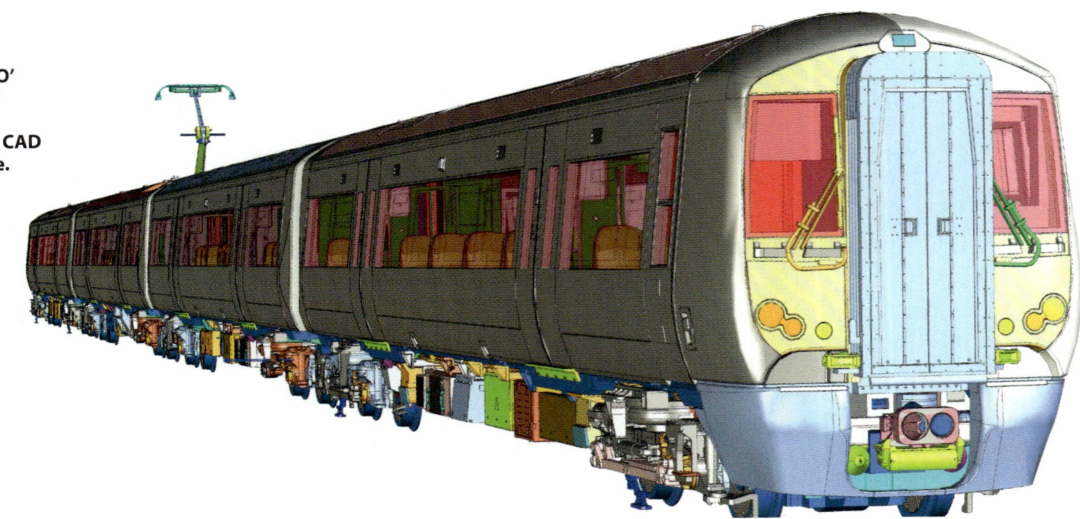

An exciting development for modern image modellers is the 'OO' gauge 'Electrostar' from Accurascale, showing the initial CAD development stage.

Bachmann's all-new Class 66 supersedes its earlier 'OO' version.

ABOVE: The Thompson 'BZ' coming in 'OO' from The Model Centre.

BELOW: Accurascale's china clay open wagons in 'OO' gauge.

The Maunsell 'U' 2-6-0 is to be issued in RTR form in 'OO' for the very first time thanks to Rapido. This is a computer generated mock-up of BR black 31620.

Heljan is joining Hornby in offering motive power in 'TT:120'. This is the Danish company's impressive 'Deltic' engineering prototype.

announced in the timeframe of this feature, models are already available (see Review of the Year).

Southern enthusiasts have had their prayers answered for a Maunsell 'U' 2-6-0, which is being developed by Rapido, paired with the later 4,000-gallon tender.

Hornby's two-decade long dominance in the Bulleid 'Light Pacific' market is finally being challenged with the Dapol and RoS 'Black Label' air-smoothed designs. These high-end models will be only available with digital bells and whistles, including sound, lights and smoke.

Accurascale will dip its feet into the steam market again with its Hunslet-design 'Austerity' 0-6-0STs. These high-specification saddle tanks are being offered in a host of livery variants including War Department, LNER, BR and industrial.

Irish steam enters the mainstream RTR market for the first time with the Great Southern Railway Class '800' 4-6-0s from Irish Railway Models (by Accurascale). The giant express engines were built for the Dublin to Cork route.

Hornby Railroad's new London South Western Railway 'B4'

0-4-0T provides an affordable option for the beginner market, while generic goods vans and open wagons are being made to match.

The revolutionised 'Santa's Express' features lighting, sound effects, USB-C charging, magnetic coupling, and dome-activated stop/start operation.

Bachmann's EFE Rail Class 74 electro-diesel locomotive fills another key gap in RTR offerings. This experimental 1960s locomotive, which combined 750V DC third rail electric equipment with diesel capability, represents an evolutionary dead-end that operated primarily on Southern Region boat train duties.

Competition in the Class 66 market is hotting up thanks to Bachmann's pitch for an all-new tooling, with enhanced deluxe variants also in development featuring tinted windows and controllable tension lock couplings.

The classic BR Class 47 is also gaining a new provider in the form of Cavelex's Brush that promises to positively bristle with detail and functions, if its acclaimed Classes 56 and 60 are anything to go by.

TABLE 6 – 'N' GAUGE NEW ROLLING STOCK PROJECTS 2025 FORWARDS			
VEHICLE	**REGION**	**MANUFACTURER**	**EXPECTED**
Pullman K Type all-steel Brake Parlour First	Various	Revolution Trains	2025
Pullman K Type all-steel Parlour First	Various	Revolution Trains	2025
Pullman K Type all-steel Parlour Third	Various	Revolution Trains	2025
Pullman K Type all-steel Kitchen First	Various	Revolution Trains	2025
Pullman K Type all-steel Kitchen Third	Various	Revolution Trains	2025
LNER Dynamometer Car	Eastern	Rapido Trains UK	TBA
GWR 'Iron Mink' van	Western	Rapido Trains UK	2025
NER P7/LNER Dia 12 coal hopper	Eastern	Graham Farish	TBA
BR 24.5ton iron ore hopper	Midland/Eastern	Revolution Trains	TBA
BR 'Borail B' bogie wagon	Various	Revolution Trains	TBA
BR 'Borail C' bogie wagon	Various	Revolution Trains	TBA
BR 'Mullet' bogie wagon	Various	Revolution Trains	TBA
BR YQA 'Parr' bogie wagon	Various	Revolution Trains	TBA
BR YQA 'Super Tench' bogie wagon	Various	Revolution Trains	TBA
FSA/FTA Freightliner container flat	Various	C-Rail	TBA
OAA air-braked open wagon	Various	Rapido Trains UK	TBA
PTA/JTA bogie tippler wagon	Various	Revolution Trains	2025
Cowans Sheldon hand crane	Various	N Gauge Society	2025
PCA alumina powder tank wagon	Eastern/Scottish	Revolution Trains	2025
TOTAL: 19			

TABLE 7 – 'OO9' GAUGE NEW PROJECTS 2025 FORWARDS			
VEHICLE	**REGION**	**MANUFACTURER**	**EXPECTED**
Vale of Rheidol 2-6-2T	Western	Revolution Trains	2026
Kerr, Stuart 'Sirdar' 0-4-0T (short-tank)	Any	Rapido Trains UK	TBA
Kerr, Stuart 'Sirdar' 0-4-0T (long-tank)	Any	Rapido Trains UK	TBA
Dropside open	Any	Rapido Trains UK	TBA
Cylindrical tank	Any	Rapido Trains UK	TBA
Gunpowder van	Any	Rapido Trains UK	TBA
Covered van	Any	Rapido Trains UK	TBA
Peaked roof van	Any	Rapido Trains UK	TBA
Manrider	Any	Rapido Trains UK	TBA
Livestock wagon	Any	Rapido Trains UK	TBA
Stake wagon	Any	Rapido Trains UK	TBA
Single-veranda brake van	Any	Rapido Trains UK	TBA
TOTAL: 12			

A beast in 'N' gauge is Sonic Model's Great Central Railway 'A5' tank engine.

Cavelex has shown off early 3D-printed samples of its forthcoming Class 47.

Accurascale and RoS have revealed plans to develop all-new 'Electrostar' Classes 375, 377, 379 and 387 EMUs.

A new budget Hornby RailRoad Class 800 IET is planned to complement the more detailed main range version.

The 1965-introduced Hunslet 0-6-0DH is the next locomotive to be announced by Revolution Trains. These industrial locomotives were first produced by the company for the N Gauge Society in 2mm:ft scale.

Imaginative rolling stock includes Hornby's BR Bulleid Tavern Cars – based on Oliver Bulleid's 'travelling pubs'

concept. Twin packs feature Diagram 2663 Kitchen Cars with Diagram 2664 Trailers in 'White Horse' (crimson and cream) and 'Jolly Tar' (BR green) variants.

Bachmann has added another Bulleid-type to its own range – the long-requested Diagram 2406 Brake Composite Corridor and Diagram 2017 Third Open.

More Southern coaches are coming in the shape of EFE's Isle of Wight-specific packs of ex-London Brighton & South Coast Railway 48ft stock.

While it has been a quieter year of locomotive hauled carriage announcements, the has been a wave of newly promised

wagon tooling.

Rapido is particularly prolific in this area with London North Western Railway 'Crystal Palace' brake vans, LNWR four-plank opens, LBSCR Billinton 10 ton brake vans (RoS exclusive) and 10-ton box vans, Great Eastern Railway five plank opens, Railway Clearing House 1907 salt wagons, Ministry of Munitions chemical tankers, LMS box vans, GWR '018' and 'N19' diagram open wagons, and Great Central Railway six-wheel 15 ton brake vans.

Phew!

Clark Railworks meanwhile has plucked for distinctive subjects – the BR bauxite-livery 'Prestwins'

(for conveyance of powdered solids) and demountable tanks.

Similarly, Oxford Rail has gone for the unusual in its choice of GWR 'Totem A'. These open frame trucks were used for moving large cast metal parts.

The Model Centre is working on a new Thompson BR Eastern Region six-wheel 'BZ' van, while Bachmann is bringing the LMS 20ton brake van into the 21st Century decades after Hornby's now ageing model was first made.

'O GAUGE'

It's been a slower year for new 7mm:1ft scale announcements,

Lionheart's reputation for high-quality 7mm:1ft scale models looks set to be upheld with its next locomotive, the Ivatt 'Mickey Mouse' tank.

with smaller steam prototypes taking centre stage.

As well as developing an Aspinal 'Pug' saddle tank in 'OO', Clark Railworks is making one in this larger gauge too – an ideal prototype for minimum space 'O' shunting layouts.

Lionheart Train's forthcoming LMS Ivatt 2-6-2T will make use of diecast metal, plastic and brass parts. Liveries include the Keighley & Worth Valley Railway's arresting red livery for 41241 while some others will be equipped with pull-push apparatus.

'N GAUGE'

It has been a similarly quieter year in 'N' gauge, but one not without its surprises, mainly from Bachmann's Graham Farish.

Its big locomotive announcement rolled two similar yet distinctive classes into one reveal: the GWR Collett 'Hall' and Hawksworth 'Modified Hall', with tooling variations to allow for the visual differences to be catered for between designs, as well as a new flat sided 4,000-gallon Hawksworth tender which is interchangeable with the Collett tender already available from Farish 'Castle' models.

Graham Farish is also adding NER P7 (LNER D12) coal hoppers to the range; as successors to the classic Stockton & Darlington Railway Chaldron waggons, Farish's pronouncement was timed to coincide with the line's 200th anniversary.

Dapol hasn't publicly declared any firm plans but is inviting expressions of interest for a new Gresley 'BG' (full brake) before committing to final production.

NARROW GAUGE

Rapido's most significant 2025 announcement is their entry into narrow gauge with the Rapido Narrow Lines brand. The 'OO9' launch features Kerr Stuart 'Sirdar' 0-4-0T locomotives and general-purpose wagons, with the brand covering all global narrow gauges and scales suggesting ambitious expansion plans.

The heavily customisable locomotive offers multiple colour options acknowledging narrow gauge individuality, while wagons feature numerous body styles representing varied rolling stock found on industrial, military, and scenic lines.

'TT:120' GAUGE

Hornby continues to lead the charge in this versatile new British scale.

This growing scale receives dedicated attention with authentic British prototypes previously unavailable in this size, demonstrating Hornby's long-term commitment to TT:120 development.

Its range expansion continues with the Brighton 'Terrier' tank engines and matching four-wheel coaches supporting pre-Grouping and Southern Railway themed layouts. The Stoudley 0-6-0Ts feature the same level of detail as their OO counterparts, scaled precisely to maintain prototype accuracy.

In an exciting new development, Danish manufacturer Heljan will be launching its own 'TT:120' range. Two models form the initial series of releases with all-new Class 55 'Deltic' Co-Co diesels and Class 122 diesel railcars. ■

'TT:120' SCALE NEW MOTIVE POWER 2025 FORWARDS			
VEHICLE	**REGION**	**MANUFACTURER**	**EXPECTED**
GWR '57XX' 0-6-0PT	Western	Hornby	TBA
GWR 'Castle' 4-6-0	Western	Hornby	TBA
LBSCR 'Terrier' 0-6-0T	Southern	Hornby	2025
LMS 'Black Five'	Midland	Hornby	TBA
LNER 'J50' 0-6-0T	Eastern	Hornby	2025
LNER 'J94' 0-6-0ST	Eastern	Hornby	TBA
BR 'Britannia' 4-6-2	Various	Hornby	TBA
BR '9F' 2-10-0	Various	Hornby	TBA
BR Class 31 A1A-A1A diesel	Various	Hornby	TBA
BR Class 37 Co-Co diesel	Various	Hornby	2025
BR Class 47 Co-Co diesel	Various	Hornby	TBA
Class 67 Co-Co diesel	Various	Hornby	TBA
BR Class 73 Co-Co electro-diesel	Various	Hornby	TBA
Class 55 'Deltic' Co-Co diesel	Eastern	Heljan	2026
Class 122 diesel railcar	Various	Heljan	2026

TOTAL: 15   STEAM: 8   DIESEL/ELECTRIC: 7

'TT:120' SCALE NEW ROLLING STOCK 2025 FORWARDS			
VEHICLE	**REGION**	**MANUFACTURER**	**EXPECTED**
GWR Collett bow-end Brake Third	Western	Hornby	TBA
GWR Collett bow-end Corridor Composite	Western	Hornby	TBA
LBSCR four-wheel Baggage Brake Third	Southern	Hornby	2025
LBSCR four-wheel Brake Third	Southern	Hornby	2025
LBSCR four-wheel First	Southern	Hornby	2025
LBSCR four-wheel Third	Southern	Hornby	2025
LNER Gresley Corridor Composite	Eastern	Hornby	TBA
LNER Gresley Corridor Brake Third	Eastern	Hornby	TBA
LMS vent van	Midland	Peco	TBA
BR 16ton open wagon	Various	Peco	TBA
BR Conflat wagon	Various	Hornby	TBA
BR Mk1 horsebox	Various	Hornby	TBA
BR 21ton mineral wagon	Various	Hornby	2025
CDA china clay hoper wagon	Various	Hornby	TBA
KFA container flat wagon	Various	Hornby	2025
MHA 'Coalfish' ballast open wagon	Various	Hornby	TBA
'Seacow' bogie ballast hopper	Various	Hornby	TBA
TTA tank wagon	Various	Hornby	TBA
VEA box van	Various	Hornby	TBA
VGA box van	Various	Hornby	TBA
MMA/JNA	Various	Revolution Trains	2025

TOTAL: 21

HORNBY TT:120
LOCOS & SETS

Official
HORNBY® TT:120
STOCKIST

The *Key Model World Shop* is proud to be an official Hornby TT:120 scale stockist. View the full collection of ready-to-run train sets, locomotives, carriages, wagons, track, accessories and buildings with exclusive images and unique video insights.

'TT:120' Branchline Freight Train Set

Cat No:
TT1005M -
£99.99
Due Autumn 2025

The Scotsman 'TT:120' Train Set

Cat No: **TT1001AM - DCC Ready: £224.99**

Inter-City 125 High Speed DCC ready Train Set

Cat No: **TT1004M - £224.99**

Inter-City 125 High Speed DCC Sound Train Set

Cat No:
TT1004M - £224.99

GNER Class 43 HST Train Pack, GNER blue

Cat No: **TT3047M (DCC ready) - £215.99**

Virgin Trains Class 43 HST Train Pack, Virgin Trains livery

Cat No: **TT3048M (DCC ready) - £215.99**

Class 66 66097, DB Schenker red and grey

Cat No:

TT3017M (DCC ready) - £143.99
TT3017TXSM (DCC sound) - £193.99

Class 66 66714 *Cromer Lifeboat*, GBRf blue

Cat No:

TT3016M (DCC ready) - £143.99

Class 66 66779 *Evening Star*, GBRf BR lined green

Cat No:

TT3018M (DCC ready) - £143.99
TT3018TXSM (DCC sound) - £193.99

Class 66 66850 *David Maidment OBE*, Colas Rail Freight

Cat No:

TT3019M (DCC ready) - £143.99
TT3019TXSM (DCC sound) - £193.99

Class 66 66789 *British Railway 1948-1997*, GBRf large logo blue

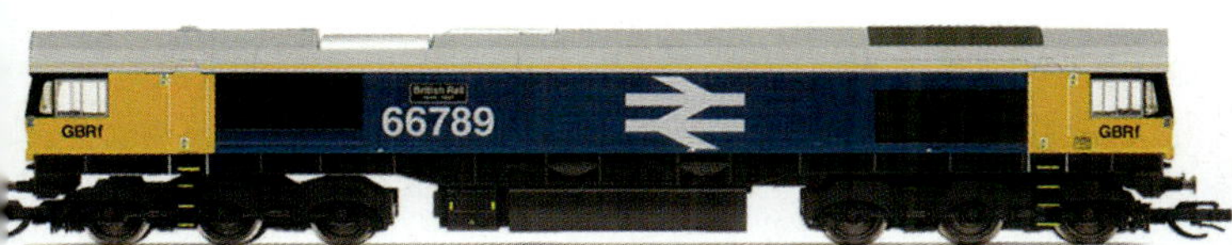

Cat No:

TT3020M (DCC ready) - £143.99

Class 08 08924, GBRf blue

Cat No:

TT3003M (DCC ready) - £124.99

CHECK OUT OUR FULL COLLECTION OF TT:120 MODELS HERE:

keymodelworld.com/shop